Author: Edward Ascoli

Proofreader: William R Schwartz

Content Review: William R Schwartz

Published by Adkins & Matchett (UK) Limited – trading as Adkins, Matchett & Toy

Second edition 2007

W9-BMH-630

UK COPYRIGHT NOTICE

Manufactured in United Kingdom

ISBN: 978-1-891112-73-7

Visit us at or buy online: www.amttraining.com

ATMM0993

AdkinsMatchett&Toy

Table of Contents

Introduction

WHAT IS A FULLY INTEGRATED MODEL?

A fully integrated model derives and projects the three main financial statements of a business over a period of up to 10 years. These are: the income statement, the balance sheet and the cash flow.

STEPS IN CREATING A MODEL

There are a number of steps that you should follow when creating a fully integrated model. These are listed below and explained in detail in subsequent sections of this reference guide:

1. Set up the model template
2. Input historical financials
3. Calculate ratios and build assumptions
4. Project the income statement
5. Project the balance sheet
6. Balance the balance sheet
7. Add interest to the income statement
8. Create a summary page

HOW TO USE THIS REFERENCE GUIDE

This workbook uses a US based fictitious company called Irene Foods to explain the steps necessary to build a fully integrated financial model in Microsoft Excel. As you work through this guide you will see extracts of Excel worksheets. Each extract will represent a different area of the model being described. A label in cell A2 of each extract indicates the area of the model that the extract represents. For example, the following is an extract from the Income Statement.

	A	B	C	D	E	F	G	H
1	Irene Foods		Hist.	Hist.	Hist.	Proj.	Proj.	Proj.
2	Income Statement		31-Dec-99	31-Dec-00	31-Dec-01	31-Dec-02	31-Dec-03	31-Dec-04
5	Depreciation		135.6	140.2	153.5	153.5	155.2	157.9
6	**Gross profit**		1,616.2	1,749.8	1,891.7	**2,031.1**	**2,182.3**	**2,343.2**
7								
8	SG&A		894.7	951.4	1,079.6	1,267.8	1,356.6	1,451.5
9	Amortisation		163.2	175.8	190.3	0.0	0.0	0.0
10	**Operating profit**		558.4	622.7	621.7	**763.2**	**825.7**	**891.6**

Both US GAAP and UK GAAP accounting terminology are used interchangeably throughout this workbook.

In order to gain full benefit from the guide, you should work through each section in the order it is presented.

Modeling Basics

This section looks at some fundamental Excel skills you will need to know before attempting to build a model.

ACCESSING THE MENU WITH THE KEYBOARD

Being able to access the menu with the keyboard will give you access to many commands quickly. You will notice that each menu item has a character that is underlined.

File	Edit	View	Insert	Format	Tools	Table	Window	Help

To access a menu item using the keyboard, hold down the ALT key and press the letter that is underlined. To access an item within a specific menu, press the letter that is underlined in the menu.

For example, to access the File, Open from the menu, hold down ALT and press the F key to access the File menu. Now to access the Open item, just press the O key (you don't have to keep ALT + F depressed in order to do this).

The following table provides a list of key menu commands to make your life easier:

Command	Shortcut
Insert a row	ALT i r
Rename a sheet	ALT o h r
Zoom your view	ALT v z
Paste Special	ALT e s
Clear all	ALT e a a
Clear Formats	ALT e a f
Fit width to cell	ALT o c a
Print Preview	ALT f v

OTHER ESSENTIAL KEYBOARD SHORTCUTS

There are a number of other keyboard shortcuts that are designed to make your life easier. The following table shows some of the main ones:

Command	Shortcut
Undo	CTRL + Z
Redo	CTRL + Y
Cut	CTRL + X
Copy	CTRL + C
Paste	CTRL + V
Goto	F5

SELECTING CELLS WITH THE STICKY SHIFT KEY

> **Sticky shift!**
>
> Hold down the SHIFT key whilst pressing one of the arrow keys (↑ ↓ ← →) to select cells with the keyboard.

Holding down the SHIFT key while pressing an arrow key enables you to select a number of contiguous cells in the direction of the arrow keys from the starting cell. This avoids the runaway mouse syndrome!

For example, to select cells A1 to E2:

	A	B	C	D	E	F
1						
2						
3						
4						

Select cell A1 to make it the starting cell. Hold down the SHIFT key and press the right arrow key 4 times and the down arrow once.

MOVING ACROSS WORKSHEETS

To move between worksheets: hold down the CTRL key and press PgDn to move one worksheet to the right or PgUp to move to one worksheet to the left.

WRITING A FORMULA WITH THE KEYBOARD

To write a formula with the keyboard:

> **Hat ^**
>
> The hat character (^) used in a formula raises a value to the power of another value. For example, 2^2 is equal to 4.

1. Type =
2. Use the arrow keys to point to the first cell reference in the formula.
3. Enter an operator (e.g. +, -, /, * or ^).
4. Use the arrow keys to point to the second cell reference in the formula.
5. Repeat steps 3 and 4 until you have completed the formula.
6. Press the ENTER key.

For example, to create a formula to calculate Gross Profit for 2003 in the worksheet below:

B4	▾	f_x =B2-B3		
	A	**B**	**C**	**D**	**E**
1		**2003**	**2004**	**2005**	**200**
2	Sales	450.0	463.5	477.4	491.7
3	COGS	315.0	324.5	334.2	344.2
4	Gross Profit	135.0			

1. Select cell B4.
2. Type =
3. Press the up arrow twice to point to B2 (cell B2 is two cells up from the formula cell).
4. Type –
5. Press the up arrow once to select cell B3 (cell B3 is one cell up from the formula cell).
6. Press ENTER.

WRITING A CROSS SHEET FORMULA WITH THE KEYBOARD

Many of your formulae will reference cells from another worksheet. These types of formulae are referred to as cross-sheet formulae and writing them by using the keyboard will save you a lot of time. To write such a formula:

1. Type =
2. Point to the cell reference using the arrow keys. If the cell is on another sheet use CTRL+ PgUp or CTRL + PgDn to go to the sheet and then use the arrow keys to point to the desired cell.
3. Type an operator (+, -, /, *, or ^).
4. Point to the second cell reference using the arrow keys. If the cell is on another sheet use CTRL + PgUp or CTRL + PgDn to go to the sheet and then use the arrow keys to point to the desired cell.
5. Repeat steps 3 and 4 until you have completed the formula.
6. Press the ENTER key.

A reference in a formula to another sheet will always have the sheet name with an explanation mark (!) followed by the cell reference. For example, when referencing cell B3 on the Income Statement sheet, the formula will be:

=Income Statement!B3

To illustrate: let's suppose you want to create a Sales growth formula on the Income Statement sheet where the % growth assumption is on a separate Assumptions sheet as shown in the worksheets below:

Assumptions   Income Statement

1. Select cell C2 on the Income Statement sheet.
2. Type =
3. Point to cell B2 on the Income Statement sheet pressing the left arrow once.
4. Type *(1+
5. Assuming that the Assumptions sheet is directly to the left of the Income Statement sheet, press CTRL + PgUp once, and use the arrow keys on your keyboard to point the correct sales growth assumption. For this example, the correct sales growth assumption is in cell C2.
6. Type)
7. Press the ENTER key.

COPYING FORMULAE

To copy a formula with the keyboard:

1.   Select the cell containing the formula.
2.   Press CTRL + C.
3.   Select the cells where you would like to copy the formula to.
4.   Press the ENTER key.

For example, to copy the Gross Profit formula in the example below:

B4	▼	f_x =B2-B3		
	A	B	C	D	E
1		2003	2004	2005	2006
2	Sales	450.0	463.5	477.4	491.7
3	COGS	315.0	324.5	334.2	344.2
4	Gross Profit	135.0	139.1	143.2	147.5
5					

1.   Select cell B4.
2.   Press CTRL + C.
3.   Hold down the SHIFT key and press the right arrow three times to select cells B4 to E4.
4.   Press the ENTER key.

MODELING FORMULAE

There are a number of modeling formulae you will encounter when building your model. The main ones are:

- Subtotals
- Growth Formulae
- % of Formulae

SUBTOTALS

We've already encountered one type of subtotal formula in our example above where we deducted COGS from Sales to arrive at Gross Profit.

B4	▼	f_x =B2-B3		
	A	B	C	D	E
1		2003	2004	2005	2006
2	Sales	450.0	463.5	477.4	491.7
3	COGS	315.0	324.5	334.2	344.2
4	Gross Profit	135.0	139.1	143.2	147.5
5					

The SUM function can be used when adding a number of different cells together. To use the SUM function:

1.   Type =SUM(
2.   Select the cells to add up.
3.   Press Enter.

For example, to calculate total expenses in the example below:

1. Select cell B10.
2. Type =SUM(
3. Select the cells to add up (remember to use the arrows and sticky SHIFT!).
4. Press Enter.

B10	▼	fx	=SUM(B6:B9)	
	A	B	C	D	E
1		2003	2004	2005	2006
2	Sales	450.0	463.5	477.4	491.7
3	COGS	315.0	324.5	334.2	344.2
4	Gross Profit	135.0	139.1	143.2	147.5
5					
6	Selling expense	13.5	13.9	14.3	14.8
7	Admin expense	15.8	16.2	16.7	17.2
8	Advertising	9.0	9.3	9.5	9.8
9	Research	15.3	15.8	16.2	16.7
10	Total Operating Expenses	53.6	55.2	56.8	58.5
11					

You can also use SUM in conjunction with another formula. For example, in the worksheet below, you can derive Gross Profit by deducting COGS and Depreciation from Sales.

B5	▼	fx	=B2-SUM(B3:B4)	
	A	B	C	D	E
1		2003	2004	2005	2006
2	Sales	450.0	463.5	477.4	491.7
3	COGS	315.0	324.5	334.2	344.2
4	Depreciation	34.0	36.0	37.0	40.0
5	Gross Profit	101.0	103.1	106.2	107.5

Sometimes, you will need to use SUM to add a non-contiguous range of cells. To do this, simply add a , [comma] between the cell ranges. In the worksheet below, we use this functionality to derive total liabilities:

B10	▼	fx	=SUM(B6,B8:B9)	
	A	B	C	D	E
1		2003	2004	2005	2006
2	**Current Liabilities**				
3	Accounts payable	2,894.0	3,100.0	3,120.0	3,450.0
4	Short-term debt	2,300.0	2,250.0	2,200.0	2,178.0
5	Taxes payable	1,500.0	1,650.0	1,649.0	1,600.0
6	**Total current liabilities**	6,694.0	7,000.0	6,969.0	7,228.0
7					
8	Long-term debt	1,200.0	1,989.0	1,978.0	1,967.0
9	Other long-term liabilities	1,000.0	1,034.0	1,045.0	1,067.0
10	**Total Liabilities**	8,894.0	10,023.0	9,992.0	10,262.0
11					

You can automatically SUM a contiguous row or column of figures using the keyboard. To do this:

1. Select the cell below a column of figures or to the right of a row of figures.
2. Hold down ALT and press =
3. Press ENTER.

When using this function, make sure that Excel has chosen the correct range before pressing ENTER!

GROWTH FORMULAE

To increase or decrease a value by a percentage, use a growth formula:

Previous value * (1 + % growth rate)

or

Previous value * (1 - % growth rate)

For example, to write a formula to grow sales in the worksheet below:

1. Select cell C3.
2. Type =
3. Press the left arrow once to point to cell B3.
4. Type *(1+
5. Press the up arrow once to point to cell C2.
6. Type)
7. Press Enter.

C3		f_x =B3*(1+C2)		
	A	B	C	D	E
1		2003	2004	2005	2006
2	Sales growth rate		8.0%	8.0%	8.0%
3	Sales	100.0	108.0		
4					

To increase or decrease a value by a quantity, simply add the quantity to the previous value or subtract the quantity from the previous value:

Previous value + quantity increase

or

Previous value – quantity increase

C3		f_x =B3+C2		
	A	B	C	D	E
1		2003	2004	2005	2006
2	Other assets $ increase		5.0	5.0	5.0
3	Sales	100.0	105.0		
4					

% OF FORMULAE

Financial models usually base most accounts on some other driver. You should use % of formulae to generate such accounts. For example, Sales is the driver of COGS. As sales increase, COGS will usually increase. As sales decrease COGS will usually decrease. Many financial models therefore project COGS as a % of sales as shown in the worksheet below:

B3   ▾   *fx* =B4*B2

	A	B	C	D	E
1		**2003**	**2004**	**2005**	**2006**
2	Sales	450.0	463.5	477.4	491.7
3	COGS	315.0	324.5	334.2	344.2
4	COGS % of Sales	70.0%	70.0%	70.0%	70.0%

BASE ANALYSIS

When you forecast a set of financial statements, you will often need to project complex accounts by separating individual increases and decreases in the account. For example, when projecting the net fixed assets (net PP&E) of a business you will want to project capital expenditure, which will increase the account and depreciation, which will decrease the account. This can be achieved using BASE analysis.

B		Amount at beginning of year
A	+	Additions during the year
S	-	Subtractions during the year
E	=	Ending amount

To set up a BASE analysis in Excel:

1. Create the BASE analysis label set. We will use net fixed assets as an example.

	A	B	C	D	E	F
1		**Net Fixed Assets**				
2		Beginning balance				
3		Capital expenditure				
4		Depreciation				
5		Ending balance				

2. Enter the ending balance of the latest historical year. In the worksheet below, this is entered in cell C5.

C5   ▾   *fx* 100

	A	B	C	D	E	F	G
1		**Net Fixed Assets**					
2		Beginning balance					
3		Capital expenditure					
4		Depreciation					
5		Ending balance	100				

3. Link the beginning balance of the first projected year to the ending balance of the previous year.

D2				f_x	=C5	
	A	B	C	D	E	F	G
1	Net Fixed Assets					
2	Beginning balance			100		
3	Capital expenditure					
4	Depreciation					
5	Ending balance		100			

4. Enter a formula to calculate the increase account and enter a formula to calculate the decrease account (information on how to create formulae for capital expenditure and depreciation is provided in subsequent sections of this workbook).

	A	B	C	D	E	F	G
1	Net Fixed Assets					
2	Beginning balance			100		
3	Capital expenditure			34		
4	Depreciation			28		
5	Ending balance		100			

5. Now create a formula to calculate the ending amount.

D5				f_x	=D2+D3-D4	
	A	B	C	D	E	F	G
1	Net Fixed Assets					
2	Beginning balance			100		
3	Capital expenditure			34		
4	Depreciation			28		
5	Ending balance		100	106		

6. Now you can copy the first projected year across to the remaining projected years. With the worksheet above, we would select cells D2:D5 and copy the formulae across.

CELL COMMENTS

Cells comments provide a useful way of documenting your work. Use these when you need to explain the contents of a cell. The more you document your work, the better!

INSERTING A CELL COMMENT

To insert a cell comment:

1. **Either:** Choose Insert, Comment from the menu.

    Or: Press SHIFT + F2.

2. Type your comment text in the text box that appears.

3. Once you have finished typing the text either click another cell with the mouse or press the ESC key.

VIEWING A CELL COMMENT

A red comment indicator shows that a cell contains a comment. To view the comment, either point to the cell containing the comment with the mouse (you don't need to click) or select the cell and press SHIFT + F2.

DELETING A CELL COMMENT

To delete a cell comment, either right click the cell containing the comment and select Delete Comment from the menu or press ALT e a m using the keyboard.

Setting up the Model Template

When setting up the template for your model, you must decide whether you want to create a single sheet model or a multi-sheet model. With a single sheet model, the different areas of the model are on one sheet. With a multi-sheet model, the different areas of the model are on several different sheets. Once you have decided which type of model to build, you should set up the formatting styles to use throughout the template.

SETTING UP THE TEMPLATE FOR A SINGLE SHEET MODEL

When setting up the template for your single sheet model, you should start by creating a header area to contain the company name, dates and so on. To do this, follow these steps:

1. Open a new workbook.
2. Make column A very narrow. This will eventually act as a very useful tool for navigating the model.
3. Type the name of the company you are forecasting in cell A1 and increase its font size to make it stand out.
4. Widen column B. This will eventually contain the line items of the model.
5. Use one column for each year starting in cell C2. Most models have 3 – 5 years of historical numbers and 5 – 10 years of projected numbers.
6. Type **Hist**. in the cell above each year that is a historical year and **Proj**. in the cell above each year that is a projected year.
7. Format your header row to make it stand out. For example, make date headings bold, add a border to the bottom of the dates and so on.
8. Freeze your header area so that when you scroll down the worksheet, you will always see the header rows. To do this, select the cell below and on the far left of the header row. In this case, select cell A3. Choose Window, Freeze Pains from the menu.

You should end up with a worksheet that looks similar to the one below:

A	B	C	D	E	F	G	H	I	J
1	Irene Foods	Hist.	Hist.	Hist.	Proj.	Proj.	Proj.	Proj.	Proj.
2		31-Dec-99	31-Dec-00	31-Dec-01	31-Dec-02	31-Dec-03	31-Dec-04	31-Dec-05	31-Dec-06
3									
4									
5									

With a single sheet model, you should organize your work into the following sections:

Assumptions

Secondary Calculations

Income Statement

Balance Sheet

Cash Flow Statement

Summary Ratios

You should enter each of the section headings in the narrow column A as illustrated below.

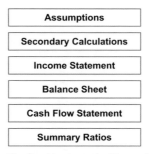

The rows between each section will eventually contain the line items of the model. You will add these line items later. At this stage, you don't need to specify the exact number of rows between each section as you can insert additional rows while building the model.

Once you have added the section headings as described above, column A acts as an extremely useful navigation bar. To see this working:

1. Select one of the section headings in column A.
2. Hold down CTRL and press the up or down arrows on your keyboard a number of times until you have reached the section you want to go to.

When your model contains all its line items, this is an invaluable trick for navigating the different sections of the model.

SETTING UP THE TEMPLATE FOR A MULTI-SHEET MODEL

With a multi-sheet model, each sheet will represent a different section of your model. To set up the template for such a model, you should firstly create the header row on one of the sheets and then copy this sheet in order to create the other sheets. This will ensure consistency and matrix integrity on all the sheets.

To create your multi-sheet template, follow these steps:

1. Open a new workbook.
2. Make column A of one of the sheets very narrow (the navigation bar is also very useful in a multi-sheet model).
3. Type the name of the company you are forecasting in cell A1 and increase its font size to make it stand out.
4. Widen column B. This will eventually contain the line items of the model.
5. Use one column for each year starting in cell C2. Most models have 3 – 5 years of historical numbers and 5 – 10 years of projected numbers.
6. Type **Hist.** in the cell above each year that is a historical year and **Proj.** in the cell above each year that is a projected year.
7. Format your header row to make it stand out. For example, make date headings bold, add a border to the bottom of the dates and so on.
8. Freeze your header area so that when you scroll down the worksheet, you will always see the header rows. To do this, select the cell below and to the left of the header row. In this case, select A3. Choose Window, Freeze Pains from the menu.

You should end up with a worksheet that looks similar to the one below:

	B	C	D	E	F	G	H	I	J
1	Irene Foods	Hist.	Hist.	Hist.	Proj.	Proj.	Proj.	Proj.	Proj.
2		31-Dec-99	31-Dec-00	31-Dec-01	31-Dec-02	31-Dec-03	31-Dec-04	31-Dec-05	31-Dec-06
3									
4									
5									

Now that you have created the model template for one of the sheets, you should copy this sheet 5 times in order to create sheets for the different sections stated above.

To copy the sheet, follow these steps:

1. Point to the sheet with the mouse pointer.

\Sheet1 / Sheet2 / Sheet3 /

2. Hold down the CTRL key and drag the sheet to the right. A little black down arrow will indicate where the copied sheet will be inserted.

3. Let go of the mouse button before the CTRL key to make a copy of the sheet. The new sheet will appear as shown below.

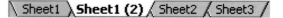

4. Repeat steps 1 – 4 from above until you have copied the desired number of sheets.

Once you have copied the sheets, you should rename each sheet so that it corresponds to a section of the model. To rename a sheet:

1. Select the sheet to rename.

2. **Either:** Press the ALT key and press o h r.

    Or: Double click the sheet tab.

3. Type the desired name.

4. Press the ENTER key.

Your template will now have sheet names to correspond to each section of the model as follows:

\ Assumptions / Calcs / Debt / IncStat / BalSheet / CashFlow \ **Summary** /

MATRIX INTEGRITY

Setting up the template for a multi-sheet model as described above is key to ensuring matrix integrity throughout the model. For example, if column F on the income statement represents the year 2002, column F on all the other sheets should also represent the year 2002. If you decide to add a new column to a worksheet of your template, make sure you remember to change the other worksheets as well.

CELL FORMATS

The worksheet cells of a well-designed model will contain the following main formats:

- Business comma
- Percent
- Historical
- Input

You should create these cell formats and save them as Styles so that they are readily available, before entering data into your model.

BUSINESS COMMA

The business comma cell format is a number format with commas as thousand separators and one decimal place. Negative numbers are displayed with brackets. This format is used to display the main financial numbers in your model. Numbers using the business format are shown below:

	A
1	100.0
2	12,500.0
3	(100.0)
4	(12,500.0)
5	

You will notice that all the decimals points are lined up, regardless of the brackets for the negative numbers.

So that you can access this format easily, you should redefine your **normal** style. Doing this will automatically format all cells in your workbook, using the business comma format. This is not a problem, as most of the cells in your model will use this style. To do this:

1. Ensure that you are in the file that you are using as your model template.

2. Choose Format Style from the menu. The Style dialog box is displayed.

Style	? X
Style name: Normal	OK
Style includes	Cancel
☑ Number General	Modify...
☑ Alignment General, Bottom Aligned	
☑ Font Times New Roman 10	Add
☑ Border No Borders	Delete
☑ Patterns No Shading	Merge...
☑ Protection Locked	

3. Make sure the Normal style is selected in the Style name box.

4. Deselect all the tick boxes with the exception of the Number tick box. This will ensure that only the number format will be applied when the style is applied to your workbook.

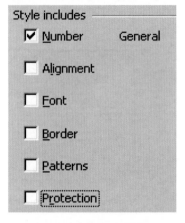

5. Select the Modify button. The Format Cells dialog box is displayed.

6. Choose the Custom category. The Format Cells dialog box will change its appearance.

Format Cells   ? ✕

| Number | Alignment | Font | Border | Patterns | Protection |

Category:

General
Number
Currency
Accounting
Date
Time
Percentage
Fraction
Scientific
Text
Special
Custom

Sample

Type:
General

General
0
0.00
#,##0
#,##0.00
#,##0;-#,##0
#,##0;[Red]-#,##0

Type the number format code, using one of the existing codes as a starting point.

OK   Cancel

7. In the Type edit box, enter the following number format:

Type:
#,##0.0_);(#,##0.0)

8. Choose OK. You will be returned to the Style dialog box. Your format code will appear next to the number check box.

☑ **Number**   #,##0.0_);(#,##0.0)

9. Choose OK on the Style dialog box to save the changes to the style. You will be returned to the worksheet.

When you enter a number into a cell, it will be formatted with the business comma format. This is because all cells in an Excel workbook use the **Normal** style by default.

PERCENT FORMAT

The Percent Format is a number formatted as a percent with one or two decimal places, depending on your preference. Negative percentages are also displayed in brackets.

Numbers entered into cells with the Percent Format are displayed with a % sign and the underlying number is divided by 100. For example, the number 0.5 is displayed as 50%. When performing calculations with such cells, Excel will use the underlying number, in this case 0.5. Numbers formatted with the percent format are displayed as follows:

	A
1	30.0%
2	130.0%
3	(30.0%)
4	(130.0%)
5	

Once again, you will notice that the decimal places line up, regardless of the brackets for negative numbers. To set this style up, modify the existing Percent Style as follows:

1. Ensure that you are in the file that you are using as your model template.

2. Choose Format Style from the menu. The Style dialog box is displayed.

3. Select the Percent style from the Style name box.

Style name:	Percent	▼

4. Deselect all the tick boxes with the exception of the Number tick box. This will ensure that only the number format will be applied when the style is applied to your workbook.

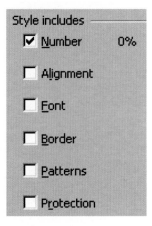

5. Select the Modify button. The Format Cells dialog box is displayed.

6.   Choose the Custom category. The Format Cells dialog box will change its appearance.

Format Cells   ? ✕

| Number | Alignment | Font | Border | Patterns | Protection |

Category:

Sample

General
Number
Currency
Accounting
Date
Time
Percentage
Fraction
Scientific
Text
Special
Custom

Type:

0%

#,##0.00;-#,##0.00
#,##0.00;[Red]-#,##0.00
£#,##0;-£#,##0
£#,##0;[Red]-£#,##0
£#,##0.00;-£#,##0.00
£#,##0.00;[Red]-£#,##0.00
0%

Type the number format code, using one of the existing codes as a starting point.

OK   Cancel

7.   In the Type box, enter the following number format:

Type:

0.0%_);(0.0%)

If you would like your percentages rounded to two decimal places, simply place two zeros after the decimal point, as shown below:

Type:

0.00%_);(0.00%)

8.   Choose OK. You will be retuned to the Style dialog box. Your format code will appear next to the number check box.

9.   Choose OK to save changes to the style and return to the worksheet.

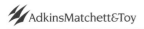

HISTORICAL NUMBERS STYLE

The Historical Numbers style will change the font color of a cell to Blue. You should use this style so that users of your model can easily distinguish between historical and projected numbers. To create this style:

1. Ensure that you are in the file that you are using as your model template.

2. Choose Format Style from the menu. The Style dialog box is displayed.

Style

Style name: Normal

Style includes
- ☑ Number   #,##0.0_);(#,##0.0)
- ☐ Alignment
- ☐ Font
- ☐ Border
- ☐ Patterns
- ☐ Protection

OK | Cancel | Modify... | Add | Delete | Merge...

3. In the Style name box, type Historical.

Style name: Historical

4. Deselect all the tick boxes with the exception of the Font tick box.

- ☐ Number
- ☐ Alignment
- ☑ Font   Airal 10
- ☐ Border
- ☐ Patterns
- ☐ Protection

5. Choose Modify. The Format Cells dialog box is displayed.

Format Cells ? X

| Number | Alignment | Font | Border | Patterns | Protection |

Category:

General
Number
Currency
Accounting
Date
Time
Percentage
Fraction
Scientific
Text
Special
Custom

Sample

Type:

#,##0.0_);(#,##0.0)

@
[h]:mm:ss
_-£* #,##0_-;-£* #,##0_-;_-£* "-"_
_-* #,##0_-;-* #,##0_-;_-* "-"_-;_-
_-£* #,##0.00_-;-£* #,##0.00_-;_
_-* #,##0.00_-;-* #,##0.00_-;_-* "
#,##0.0_);(#,##0.0)

Type the number format code, using one of the existing codes as a starting point.

OK   Cancel

6. Select the Font tab.

Format Cells ? X

| Number | Alignment | Font | Border | Patterns | Protection |

Font:

Airal

Abadi MT Condensed Li
Albertus Extra Bold
Albertus Medium
Antique Olive

Font style:

Regular

Regular
Italic
Bold
Bold Italic

Size:

10

8
9
10
11

Underline:

None

Color:

Automatic

Effects

☐ Strikethrough
☐ Superscript
☐ Subscript

Preview

AaBbCcYyZz

This font is not installed on the system. The closest available font will be used for printing.

OK   Cancel

7.   Select the Blue color using the Color drop down arrow as illustrated below.

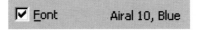

8.   Choose OK. You will be returned to the Styles dialog box. The Blue font format will be indicated to the right of the Font option.

☑ Font   Airal 10, Blue

9.   Choose OK to add the new style.

INPUT STYLE

An Input style should be created and used for the assumptions of your model. Users will know that they can enter new values into the input cells, without destroying the formula engineering behind the model. The Input style has the following properties: cell color is light yellow; font color is blue; and the cell has a border. To create an input style:

1.   Ensure that you are in the file that you are using as your model template.

2. Choose Format Style from the menu. The Style dialog box is displayed.

3. In the Style name box, type Input.

4. Deselect all the tick boxes, with the exception of Font, Borders and Patterns.

5. Choose <u>M</u>odify. The Format cells dialog box is displayed.

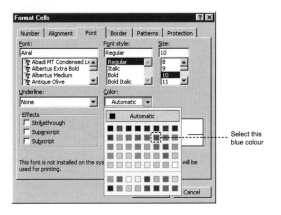

6. Go to the Font tab and choose the Blue color.

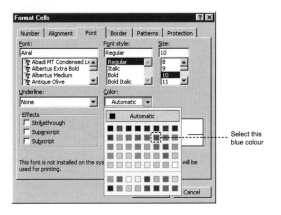

Select this blue colour

7. Go to the Border tab and choose a thin line style followed by the Outline button.

8. Go to the Patterns tab and choose a light yellow color.

9. Choose OK. You will be returned to the Style dialog box.

10. Choose OK to add the style. You will be returned to the worksheet.

APPLYING A STYLE TO A CELL

In order to apply a style to a cell:

1. Select the desired cell or range of cells.
2. Choose Format, Style from the menu.
3. Select the desired style from the Style name drop down list.
4. Choose OK.

Sometimes you will want to apply more than one style to the same cell. For example, suppose one of your input assumptions is a percentage. In this case you will need to apply both the Percent style and Input style to the cell or range of cells.

Styles can be applied to your worksheet much more quickly by adding the Style box to one of your toolbars. To do this:

1. Choose Tools, Customize from the menu. The Customize dialog box is displayed.

2. Choose the Commands tab.

3. Select the Format category and click and drag the Style command to a desired location on one of your existing toolbars.

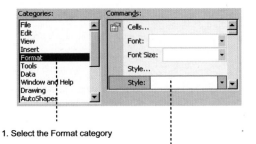

1. Select the Format category

2. Click and drag Style command to desired location on existing toolbar

4. Choose Close.

The Style Box will appear on your toolbar as illustrated below. To select a style:

1. Select the cell to apply the style to.

2. Hold down the ALT key and press the apostrophe ['] key. This will activate the Style Box.

3. **Either:** Use the up and down arrows to select the desired style.

   Or: Type the first letter of the style. For example, to select the Input style, type I. Or to select the Percent style, type P.

4. Press the Enter key to apply the style.

Shortcut!

Press ALT + **'to activate the style box on the toolbar.** *(you must add the style box to your toolbar before you can use this feature).*

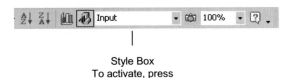

Style Box
To activate, press
ALT + '

MERGING STYLES

Styles only exist in the file that you created them in. You will therefore not be able to use the styles you created in one file in another file unless you import the styles from the source file. This is called Merging styles. To import or Merge styles:

1. Ensure that both the file containing the styles (source file) and the file to receive the styles (destination file) are open.

2. Go to the destination file.

3. Choose Format, Style. The style dialog box is displayed.

4. Choose the Merge button. The Merge dialog box is displayed. This dialog box contains a list of all currently open Excel files.

```
Merge Styles                        [?][X]

Merge styles from:

Hershey.XLS                          [▲]



                                     [▼]

              [   OK   ]   [  Cancel  ]
```

5. Select the file containing the styles to import.

6. Choose OK. If styles in the source file have the same names as styles in the destination file, the following dialog box is displayed:

```
Microsoft Excel                        [X]

   (i)   Merge styles that have the same names?

      [  Yes  ]   [  No  ]   [ Cancel ]
```

7. **Either:** Choose Yes to replace styles in the destination file with styles in the source file that have the same name.

   Or: Choose No to only import those styles with unique names.

8. Choose OK to close the Style dialog box and return to the worksheet.

Input Historical Numbers

An integrated model will normally contain 3 - 5 years of historical income statement and balance sheet information, with approximately the same line items as the available historical statements of the business to be analyzed.

INPUTTING INCOME STATEMENT HISTORICAL NUMBERS

The income statement of your model should have approximately the same line items as the income statement of the business's published financial reports. However, there are a number of accounts that should be forecast separately and should therefore have their own line item. These accounts are normally:

- Depreciation
- Amortization
- Interest Income
- Interest Expense

DEPRECIATION

Unless stated otherwise, the depreciation expense in a company's published income statement will normally be included in the cost of sales account and overhead expense accounts such as SG&A. If the business is a manufacturing company, the majority of the depreciation will be in cost of sales. If the company is a service-oriented business, the majority of the deprecation will be in the overhead accounts.

When modeling an income statement of a business, you must make an informed decision as to where the majority of the depreciation is located, based on the rule stated above. You must then remove the depreciation from this account and put it on its own line item in your model. The process of removing the depreciation from an account is referred to as "cleaning" the account.

When cleaning an account, you must give as much information as necessary to a potential user of your model as to how you cleaned the account. For example, if a manufacturing company's cost of goods sold was 1,000 and the depreciation expense was 90 in one of the historical years, its clean cost of goods sold would be 910. Rather than simply typing 910 for the clean cost of goods sold, you should write a simple formula as follows:

= 1000 – 90

This will indicate to a potential user what you have done with the cost of goods sold line when they are comparing your model to the published financial statements.

You will normally find the depreciation charge for the year in the operating section of the cash flow or the fixed asset footnote in the company's published financial reports.

Harry's Chocolate Manufacturer

Harry's Chocolates is a business that manufactures a variety of confectionary products. You are in the process of modeling its income statement. The following are extracts from Harry's published income statement:

	2000	2001	2002
Sales	450	470	490
Cost of sales	300	310	320
Gross profit	150	160	170

Depreciation charge for 2000, 2001 and 2002 is 20, 25 and 30 respectively.

As Harry's Chocolates is a manfacturing company, you decide that most of the depreciation will be in the costs of sales account of Harry's published financial statements. Your modeled income statement will therefore look as follows:

E4		▼	f_x	=320-30
A	B	C	D	E
1 **Harry's Chocolates**		Hist.	Hist.	Hist.
2 **Income Statement**		**Dec-00**	**Dec-01**	**Dec-02**
3 Sales		450.0	470.0	490.0
4 Clean cost of sales		280.0	285.0	290.0
5 Depreciation		20.0	25.0	30.0
6 **Gross Profit**		**150.0**	**160.0**	**170.0**

Your modeled income statement should contain a clean cost of sales line and a separate depreciation line, all above the Gross Profit line. Also notice how a simple formula has been used to work out the clean cost of sales line. In the worksheet above you can see that the formula =320 – 30 has been used to calculate clean cost of sales for 2002. This has also been done for 2001 and 2000.

AMORTIZATION

Unless stated otherwise, amortization will normally be included in one of the overhead cost accounts on a company's published income statement. Amortization expense can be found in the published cash flow statement or the intangibles footnote.

Similar to depreciation, amortization on the modeled income statement should be forecast separately in its own line item and the cost account originally containing amortization should be cleaned. As with depreciation, formulae should be included in the cost line item to make this as clear as possible.

INTEREST INCOME AND INTEREST EXPENSE

The interest line item on a company's published income statement will normally be interest expense net of interest income. However, sometimes you will find that interest expense will be disclosed separately on the face of the published income statement and interest income will be included in another income or other expense account.

In a financial model, interest expense and interest income should be forecast separately. They should therefore have their own line items. Once again, when cleaning the various accounts to derive interest income and expense, you should make your calculations explicit by using formulae in the various line items.

PUTTING IT ALL TOGETHER

Once you have added the line items and input the historical numbers, a typical income statement for a US company will look similar to the one illustrated below:

	B	C	D	E
		Hist.	Hist.	Hist.
1 Irene Foods				
2 Income Statement		31-Dec-99	31-Dec-00	31-Dec-01
3	Net Sales	3,970.9	4,221.0	4,557.2
4	Clean COGS	2,219.2	2,331.0	2,512.1
5	Depreciation	135.6	140.2	153.5
6	**Gross profit**	1,616.2	1,749.8	1,891.7
7				
8	SG&A	894.7	951.4	1,079.6
9	Amortisation	163.2	175.8	190.3
10	**Operating profit**	558.4	622.7	621.7
11				
12	Non-recurring items	(243.8)	0.0	209.1
13	Interest Income	3.0	4.9	2.4
14	Interest Expense	77.3	81.0	71.5
15	**Profit before taxes**	727.9	546.6	343.6
16				
17	Taxes	267.6	212.1	136.4
18	**Net income**	460.3	334.5	207.2
19				
20	**Shareholder information**			
21	Basic weighted average shares outstanding	140.0	137.3	136.2
22	Diluted weighted average shares outstanding	141.3	138.4	137.7
23	Basic earnings per share	$3.29	$2.44	$1.52
24	Diluted earnings per share	$3.26	$2.42	$1.50
25	Basic dividends per share	$1.00	$1.06	$1.14

INPUTTING BALANCE SHEET HISTORICAL NUMBERS

The balance sheet should have approximately the same line items as the company's published balance sheet. Depending on the purpose of the model, you will sometimes consolidate some of the published line items into other assets or other liability accounts. When doing this, remember to include formulae and cell comments so that future users of your model can see what you have done.

A typical balance sheet will look as follows:

	A	B	C	D	E
1	Irene Foods		Hist.	Hist.	Hist.
2	Balance Sheet		31-Dec-99	31-Dec-00	31-Dec-01
3	Assets				
4	Current assets				
5	Excess Cash				
6	Cash and cash equivalents			32.0	134.1
7	Accounts receivable			379.7	361.7
8	Inventories			605.2	512.1
9	Deferred income taxes			76.1	96.9
10	Prepaid expenses and other			202.4	62.6
11	Total current assets			1,295.3	1,167.5
12					
13	Non-current assets				
14	Net PP&E			1,585.4	1,534.9
15	Goodwill			474.4	429.1
16	Other assets			92.6	115.9
17	Total assets			3,447.8	3,247.4
18					
19	Liabilities				
20	Current liabilities				
21	Revolver				
22	Accounts payable			149.2	133.0
23	Accrued liabilities			358.1	462.9
24	Accrued income taxes			1.5	2.6
25	Other short-term debt			257.6	7.0
26	Total current liabilities			766.4	605.5
27					
28	Non-current liabilities				
29	Total long-term debt			878.2	877.9
30	Other long-term liabilities			327.7	361.0
31	Deferred income taxes			300.5	255.8
32	Total liabilities			2,272.7	2,100.2
33					
34	Equity				
35	Common stock			180.0	180.0
36	Additional paid in capital			13.1	3.3
37	Retained earnings			2,627.1	2,653.2
38	Treasury stock			(1,645.1)	(1,689.2)
39	Total equity			1,175.0	1,147.2
40	Total liabilities & equity			3,447.8	3,247.4

You should also input capital expenditure historical values into your model. To do this, set up a fixed asset (PP&E) schedule in the calculations section of the model and input the capital expenditure values in the appropriate cells as shown below:

	A	B	C	D	E
1	Irene Foods		Hist.	Hist.	Hist.
2	Calculations		31-Dec-99	31-Dec-00	31-Dec-01
3	PP&E				
4	Net PP&E, beginning balance				
5	Capital expenditures		140.8	143.0	170.0
6	Annual depreciation				
7	Net PP&E, ending balance				

Historical capital expenditure values can be found in the cash flow statement of the published financial reports.

You will complete the remaining parts of the fixed asset (PP&E) schedule when forecasting the income statement (profit and loss account).

Calculating Ratios and Building Assumptions

CALCULATING RATIOS

Ratios should be calculated based on the historical financial data you input into your model. They should be calculated in the assumptions area and should be divided into groups, such as:

- Income statement
- Current assets
- Non-current assets
- Current liabilities
- Non-current liabilities
- Equity

A typical model will contain the following ratios shown in the worksheet below. You will notice that some ratios are missing from some of the historical years. This is because information was not available from the annual report when building this model.

	A B	C	D	E
		Hist.	Hist.	Hist.
1	Irene Foods	31-Dec-99	31-Dec-00	31-Dec-01
2	Assumptions			
3	*Income statement*			
4	Sales growth		6.3%	8.0%
5	Clean COGS as % of sales	55.9%	55.2%	55.1%
6	Annual depr. as % of previous PPE			9.7%
7	SG&A as % of sales	22.5%	22.5%	23.7%
8	Amortisation amount	163.2	175.8	190.3
9	Non-recurring items amount	(243.8)	0.0	209.1
10	Effective tax rate	36.8%	38.8%	39.7%
11	*Shareholder info*			
12	Basic weighted average shares outstanding	140.0	137.3	136.2
13	Diluted weighted average shares outstanding	141.3	138.4	137.7
14	Dividend per share growth rate		5.1%	7.7%
15	*Balance sheet: current assets*			
16	Cash & cash equivalents % of sales		0.8%	2.9%
17	Accounts receivable as % of sales		9.0%	7.9%
18	Inventories % of COGS		26.0%	20.4%
19	Deferred income tax asset % of sales		1.8%	2.1%
20	Prepaid expenses and other % of sales		4.8%	1.4%
21	*Balance sheet: non-current assets*			
22	Capital expenditures % of sales	3.5%	3.4%	3.7%
23	Other assets % of sales		2.2%	2.5%
24	*Balance sheet: liabilities*			
25	Accounts payable % of COGS		6.4%	5.3%
26	Accrued liabilities % of sales		8.5%	10.2%
27	Accrued income taxes % of tax expense		0.7%	1.9%
28	Other long-term liabilities % of sales		7.8%	7.9%
29	Long-term deferred tax liability % of sales		7.1%	5.6%
30	*Balance sheet: equity*			
31	Common stock		180.0	180.0
32	Additional paid in capital		13.1	3.3
33	Share repurchases $ amount			

BUILDING ASSUMPTIONS

Assumptions are the inputs that drive the various accounts in the model. The cells containing the assumptions should be formatted using the Input style (see Input style, page 24) so that a user of the model can easily identify them as inputs.

Projecting the Income Statement

SALES/REVENUE

The sales / revenue line is the first line item to be projected on the income statement using a growth formula as follows:

= previous year sales * (1 + % growth assumption)

It is this line that will drive many of the other accounts in the model as we are building a sales driven model.

F3	▼	f_x	=E3*(1+Assumptions!F4)				
A	B	C	D	E	F	G	H
1 Irene Foods		Hist.	Hist.	Hist.	Proj.	Proj.	Proj.
2 Income Statement		31-Dec-99	31-Dec-00	31-Dec-01	31-Dec-02	31-Dec-03	31-Dec-04
3 Net Sales		3,970.9	4,221.0	4,557.2	4,876.2	5,217.6	5,582.8

COST OF SALES (COGS)

The cost of sales line is normally projected as a % of sales. The following formula should be used:

= COGS % of sales assumption * Sales

F4	▼	f_x	=Assumptions!F5*IncState!F3				
A	B	C	D	E	F	G	H
1 Irene Foods		Hist.	Hist.	Hist.	Proj.	Proj.	Proj.
2 Income Statement		31-Dec-99	31-Dec-00	31-Dec-01	31-Dec-02	31-Dec-03	31-Dec-04
3 Net Sales		3,970.9	4,221.0	4,557.2	4,876.2	5,217.6	5,582.8
4 Clean COGS		2,219.2	2,331.0	2,512.1	2,691.7	2,880.1	3,081.7

DEPRECIATION

The depreciation should be derived in the calculations area of the model along with capital expenditure. To derive depreciation:

1. Go to the calculations section of your model and ensure that you have the following schedule set up. You should have set this up when inputting the capital expenditure historical values into the model.

	A	B	C	D	E
1	Irene Foods		Hist.	Hist.	Hist.
2	Calculations		31-Dec-99	31-Dec-00	31-Dec-01
3	PP&E				
4	Net PP&E, beginning balance				
5	Capital expenditures		140.8	143.0	170.0
6	Annual depreciation				
7	Net PP&E, ending balance				

2. You should have already input the historical fixed asset (PP&E) balances on the balance sheet. Now you must link them into the fixed assets (PP&E) ending balances in the fixed asset schedule of the calculations area of the model.

	E7			f_x	=BalSheet!E14

	A — B	C	D	E	
1	Irene Foods	Hist.	Hist.	Hist.	
2	Calculations	31-Dec-99	31-Dec-00	31-Dec-01	31-…
3	PP&E				
4	Net PP&E, beginning balance				1
5	Capital expenditures	140.8	143.0	170.0	
6	Annual depreciation				
7	Net PP&E, ending balance			1,534.9	1

3. Link the beginning PP&E balance of the first projected year to the ending PP&E balance of the previous year.

	F4			f_x	=E7

	A — B	C	D	E	F
1	Irene Foods	Hist.	Hist.	Hist.	Proj.
2	Calculations	31-Dec-99	31-Dec-00	31-Dec-01	31-Dec-02
3	PP&E				
4	Net PP&E, beginning balance				1,534.9
5	Capital expenditures	140.8	143.0	170.0	
6	Annual depreciation				
7	Net PP&E, ending balance			1,534.9	

4. Write a formula to calculate capital expenditure in the first projected year. The formula should be a % of sales formula:

	F5			f_x	=Assumptions!F22*IncState!F3

	A — B	C	D	E	F	G	H
1	Irene Foods	Hist.	Hist.	Hist.	Proj.	Proj.	Proj.
2	Calculations	31-Dec-99	31-Dec-00	31-Dec-01	31-Dec-02	31-Dec-03	31-Dec-04
3	PP&E						
4	Net PP&E, beginning balance				1,534.9		
5	Capital expenditures	140.8	143.0	170.0	170.7		
6	Annual depreciation						
7	Net PP&E, ending balance			1,534.9			

5. Write a formula to calculate depreciation in the first projected year. You will see from the assumptions that this model projects depreciation as a % of the beginning fixed asset (PP&E) balance.

	F6			f_x	=Assumptions!F6*Calcs!E7

	A — B	C	D	E	F	G	H
1	Irene Foods	Hist.	Hist.	Hist.	Proj.	Proj.	Proj.
2	Calculations	31-Dec-99	31-Dec-00	31-Dec-01	31-Dec-02	31-Dec-03	31-Dec-04
3	PP&E						
4	Net PP&E, beginning balance				1,534.9		
5	Capital expenditures	140.8	143.0	170.0	170.7		
6	Annual depreciation				153.5		
7	Net PP&E, ending balance			1,534.9			

6. Calculate the ending PP&E balance for the first projected year. This should be done using the following formula:

= beg. PP&E + Capex – Dep'n

F7			f_x	=F4+F5-F6	
	A B	C	D	E	F
1	**Irene Foods**	Hist.	Hist.	Hist.	Proj.
2	**Calculations**	31-Dec-99	31-Dec-00	31-Dec-01	31-Dec-02 31-
3	**PP&E**				
4	Net PP&E, beginning balance				1,534.9
5	Capital expenditures	140.8	143.0	170.0	170.7
6	Annual depreciation				153.5
7	Net PP&E, ending balance			1,534.9	1,552.1

7. Now select cell F4:F7 and copy the formulae across in one go!

	A B	C	D	E	F	G	H	I
1	Irene Foods	Hist.	Hist.	Hist.	Proj.	Proj.	Proj.	Proj.
2	Calculations	31-Dec-99	31-Dec-00	31-Dec-01	31-Dec-02	31-Dec-03	31-Dec-04	31-Dec-05
3	PP&E							
4	Net PP&E, beginning balance				1,534.9	1,552.1	1,579.5	1,616.9
5	Capital expenditures	140.8	143.0	170.0	170.7	182.6	195.4	209.1
6	Annual depreciation				153.5	155.2	157.9	161.7
7	Net PP&E, ending balance			1,534.9	1,552.1	1,579.5	1,616.9	1,664.3

Once you have derived the depreciation, you can link this into the income statement as shown below:

F5			f_x	=Calcs!F6			
	A B	C	D	E	F	G	H
1	Irene Foods	Hist.	Hist.	Hist.	Proj.	Proj.	Proj.
2	Income Statement	31-Dec-99	31-Dec-00	31-Dec-01	31-Dec-02	31-Dec-03	31-Dec-04
3	Net Sales	3,970.9	4,221.0	4,557.2	4,876.2	5,217.6	5,582.8
4	Clean COGS	2,219.2	2,331.0	2,512.1	2,691.7	2,880.1	3,081.7
5	Depreciation	135.6	140.2	153.5	153.5	155.2	157.9

GROSS PROFIT

To derive gross profit, subtract clean cogs and depreciation from sales. This can be done using the following formula:

F6			f_x	=F3-SUM(F4:F5)		
	A B	C	D	E	F	G
1	Irene Foods	Hist.	Hist.	Hist.	Proj.	Proj.
2	Income Statement	31-Dec-99	31-Dec-00	31-Dec-01	31-Dec-02	31-Dec-03
3	Net Sales	3,970.9	4,221.0	4,557.2	4,876.2	5,217.6
4	Clean COGS	2,219.2	2,331.0	2,512.1	2,691.7	2,880.1
5	Depreciation	135.6	140.2	153.5	153.5	155.2
6	**Gross profit**	1,616.2	1,749.8	1,891.7	2,031.1	2,182.3

SG&A

SG&A costs are normally projected as a % of sales.

= SG&A % of sales assumption * Sales

F8			f_x	=Assumptions!F7*IncState!F3		
	A B	C	D	E	F	G	H
1	Irene Foods	Hist.	Hist.	Hist.	Proj.	Proj.	Proj.
2	Income Statement	31-Dec-99	31-Dec-00	31-Dec-01	31-Dec-02	31-Dec-03	31-Dec-04
3	Net Sales	3,970.9	4,221.0	4,557.2	4,876.2	5,217.6	5,582.8
4	Clean COGS	2,219.2	2,331.0	2,512.1	2,691.7	2,880.1	3,081.7
5	Depreciation	135.6	140.2	153.5	153.5	155.2	157.9
6	**Gross profit**	1,616.2	1,749.8	1,891.7	2,031.1	2,182.3	2,343.2
7							
8	SG&A	894.7	951.4	1,079.6	1,267.8	1,356.6	1,451.5

AMORTIZATION

Amortization on the income statement can be linked to the amortization amount in the assumptions area of the model.

F9		fx	=Assumptions!F8			

	B	C	D	E	F	G	H
1	**Irene Foods**	*Hist.*	*Hist.*	*Hist.*	*Proj.*	*Proj.*	*Proj.*
2	**Income Statement**	*31-Dec-99*	*31-Dec-00*	*31-Dec-01*	*31-Dec-02*	*31-Dec-03*	*31-Dec-04*
3	Net Sales	3,970.9	4,221.0	4,557.2	4,876.2	5,217.6	5,582.8
4	Clean COGS	2,219.2	2,331.0	2,512.1	2,691.7	2,880.1	3,081.7
5	Depreciation	135.6	140.2	153.5	153.5	155.2	157.9
6	**Gross profit**	1,616.2	1,749.8	1,891.7	**2,031.1**	**2,182.3**	**2,343.2**
7							
8	SG&A	894.7	951.4	1,079.6	1,267.8	1,356.6	1,451.5
9	Amortisation	163.2	175.8	190.3	0.0	0.0	0.0

OPERATING PROFIT

Operating profit is derived by subtracting SG&A and amortization from gross profit.

F10		fx	=F6-SUM(F8:F9)		

	B	C	D	E	F	G
1	**Irene Foods**	*Hist.*	*Hist.*	*Hist.*	*Proj.*	*Proj.*
2	**Income Statement**	*31-Dec-99*	*31-Dec-00*	*31-Dec-01*	*31-Dec-02*	*31-Dec-03*
3	Net Sales	3,970.9	4,221.0	4,557.2	4,876.2	5,217.6
4	Clean COGS	2,219.2	2,331.0	2,512.1	2,691.7	2,880.1
5	Depreciation	135.6	140.2	153.5	153.5	155.2
6	**Gross profit**	1,616.2	1,749.8	1,891.7	**2,031.1**	**2,182.3**
7						
8	SG&A	894.7	951.4	1,079.6	1,267.8	1,356.6
9	Amortisation	163.2	175.8	190.3	0.0	0.0
10	**Operating profit**	558.4	622.7	621.7	**763.2**	**825.7**

NON-RECURRING ITEMS

Non-recurring items can not be projected. However, at times companies may estimate some major upcoming non-recurring items that they foresee in the near future (i.e. planned severance or restructuring charges). With the exception of these announced non-recurring items, your assumption for non-recurring items should be zero during the projection period.

F12		fx	=Assumptions!F9	

	B	C	D	E	F
1	**Irene Foods**	*Hist.*	*Hist.*	*Hist.*	*Proj.*
2	**Income Statement**	*31-Dec-99*	*31-Dec-00*	*31-Dec-01*	*31-Dec-02*
3	Net Sales	3,970.9	4,221.0	4,557.2	4,876.2
4	Clean COGS	2,219.2	2,331.0	2,512.1	2,691.7
5	Depreciation	135.6	140.2	153.5	153.5
6	**Gross profit**	1,616.2	1,749.8	1,891.7	**2,031.1**
7					
8	SG&A	894.7	951.4	1,079.6	1,267.8
9	Amortisation	163.2	175.8	190.3	0.0
10	**Operating profit**	558.4	622.7	621.7	**763.2**
11					
12	Non-recurring items	(243.8)	0.0	209.1	0.0

INTEREST INCOME AND EXPENSE

Interest income and expense should be the very last thing that is calculated in the model. It should therefore be left blank until the other parts of the model are complete.

	A B	C	D	E	F
1	Irene Foods	Hist.	Hist.	Hist.	Proj.
2	Income Statement	31-Dec-99	31-Dec-00	31-Dec-01	31-Dec-02
3	Net Sales	3,970.9	4,221.0	4,557.2	4,876.2
4	Clean COGS	2,219.2	2,331.0	2,512.1	2,691.7
5	Depreciation	135.6	140.2	153.5	153.5
6	Gross profit	1,616.2	1,749.8	1,891.7	2,031.1
7					
8	SG&A	894.7	951.4	1,079.6	1,267.8
9	Amortisation	163.2	175.8	190.3	0.0
10	Operating profit	558.4	622.7	621.7	763.2
11					
12	Non-recurring items	(243.8)	0.0	209.1	0.0
13	Interest Income	3.0	4.9	2.4	
14	Interest Expense	77.3	81.0	71.5	

PROFIT BEFORE TAXES

Profit before taxes (PBT) is derived using the following formula:

Operating profit – non recurring items + int. inc – int. exp

F15		f_x	=F10-F12+F13-F14		

	A B	C	D	E	F
1	Irene Foods	Hist.	Hist.	Hist.	Proj.
2	Income Statement	31-Dec-99	31-Dec-00	31-Dec-01	31-Dec-02
3	Net Sales	3,970.9	4,221.0	4,557.2	4,876.2
4	Clean COGS	2,219.2	2,331.0	2,512.1	2,691.7
5	Depreciation	135.6	140.2	153.5	153.5
6	Gross profit	1,616.2	1,749.8	1,891.7	2,031.1
7					
8	SG&A	894.7	951.4	1,079.6	1,267.8
9	Amortisation	163.2	175.8	190.3	0.0
10	Operating profit	558.4	622.7	621.7	763.2
11					
12	Non-recurring items	(243.8)	0.0	209.1	0.0
13	Interest Income	3.0	4.9	2.4	
14	Interest Expense	77.3	81.0	71.5	
15	Profit before taxes	727.9	546.6	343.6	763.2

TAX

Tax expense can be calculated by multiplying the tax rate assumption by profit before taxes.

F17		f_x	=Assumptions!F10*IncState!F15			

	A B	C	D	E	F	G	H
1	Irene Foods	Hist.	Hist.	Hist.	Proj.	Proj.	Proj.
2	Income Statement	31-Dec-99	31-Dec-00	31-Dec-01	31-Dec-02	31-Dec-03	31-Dec-04
3	Net Sales	3,970.9	4,221.0	4,557.2	4,876.2	5,217.6	5,582.8
4	Clean COGS	2,219.2	2,331.0	2,512.1	2,691.7	2,880.1	3,081.7
5	Depreciation	135.6	140.2	153.5	153.5	155.2	157.9
6	Gross profit	1,616.2	1,749.8	1,891.7	2,031.1	2,182.3	2,343.2
7							
8	SG&A	894.7	951.4	1,079.6	1,267.8	1,356.6	1,451.5
9	Amortisation	163.2	175.8	190.3	0.0	0.0	0.0
10	Operating profit	558.4	622.7	621.7	763.2	825.7	891.6
11							
12	Non-recurring items	(243.8)	0.0	209.1	0.0	0.0	0.0
13	Interest Income	3.0	4.9	2.4			
14	Interest Expense	77.3	81.0	71.5			
15	Profit before taxes	727.9	546.6	343.6	763.2	825.7	891.6
16							
17	Taxes	267.6	212.1	136.4	305.3	330.3	356.6

NET INCOME

Net income is derived by subtracting taxes from profit before taxes.

F18				f_x	=F15-F17

	A	B	C	D	E	F
1	Irene Foods		Hist.	Hist.	Hist.	Proj.
2	Income Statement		31-Dec-99	31-Dec-00	31-Dec-01	31-Dec-02
3	Net Sales		3,970.9	4,221.0	4,557.2	4,876.2
4	Clean COGS		2,219.2	2,331.0	2,512.1	2,691.7
5	Depreciation		135.6	140.2	153.5	153.5
6	Gross profit		1,616.2	1,749.8	1,891.7	2,031.1
7						
8	SG&A		894.7	951.4	1,079.6	1,267.8
9	Amortisation		163.2	175.8	190.3	0.0
10	Operating profit		558.4	622.7	621.7	763.2
11						
12	Non-recurring items		(243.8)	0.0	209.1	0.0
13	Interest Income		3.0	4.9	2.4	
14	Interest Expense		77.3	81.0	71.5	
15	Profit before taxes		727.9	546.6	343.6	763.2
16						
17	Taxes		267.6	212.1	136.4	305.3
18	Net income		460.3	334.5	207.2	457.9

SHAREHOLDER INFORMATION

The shareholder information section should present basic and diluted
average shares outstanding, basic and diluted earnings per share
and dividend per share information. You should place this under the
income statement.

		C	D	E	F
20	Shareholder information				
21	Basic weighted average shares outstanding	140.0	137.3	136.2	136.2
22	Diluted weighted average shares outstanding	141.3	138.4	137.7	137.7
23	Basic earnings per share	$3.29	$2.44	$1.52	$3.36	$3.64
24	Diluted earnings per share	$3.26	$2.42	$1.50	$3.33	$3.60
25	Dividend per share	$1.00	$1.06	$1.14	$1.22	$1.30

BASIC AND DILUTED SHARES OUTSTANDING

You should include basic and diluted shares outstanding as
constants in the assumptions area of the model and link them to the
shareholder information section of the income statement. You should
keep these numbers flat during the projection period, as it is not
possible to forecast basic and diluted shares outstanding.

F21				f_x	=Assumptions!F12

	A	B	C	D	E	F
1	Irene Foods		Hist.	Hist.	Hist.	Proj.
2	Income Statement		31-Dec-99	31-Dec-00	31-Dec-01	31-Dec-02
3	Net Sales		3,970.9	4,221.0	4,557.2	4,876.2
4	Clean COGS		2,219.2	2,331.0	2,512.1	2,691.7
5	Depreciation		135.6	140.2	153.5	153.5
6	Gross profit		1,616.2	1,749.8	1,891.7	2,031.1
7						
8	SG&A		894.7	951.4	1,079.6	1,267.8
9	Amortisation		163.2	175.8	190.3	0.0
10	Operating profit		558.4	622.7	621.7	763.2
11						
12	Non-recurring items		(243.8)	0.0	209.1	0.0
13	Interest Income		3.0	4.9	2.4	
14	Interest Expense		77.3	81.0	71.5	
15	Profit before taxes		727.9	546.6	343.6	763.2
16						
17	Taxes		267.6	212.1	136.4	305.3
18	Net income		460.3	334.5	207.2	457.9
19						
20	Shareholder information					
21	Basic weighted average shares outstanding		140.0	137.3	136.2	136.2
22	Diluted weighted average shares outstanding		141.3	138.4	137.7	137.7

BASIC AND DILUTED EARNINGS PER SHARE (EPS)

Basic EPS is derived by dividing the earnings available to common shareholders by the basic number of shares outstanding.

F23		f_x =F18/F21			
	B	C	D	E	F
A		Hist.	Hist.	Hist.	Proj.
1 Irene Foods		31-Dec-99	31-Dec-00	31-Dec-01	31-Dec-02
2 Income Statement					
3 Net Sales		3,970.9	4,221.0	4,557.2	4,876.2
4 Clean COGS		2,219.2	2,331.0	2,512.1	2,691.7
5 Depreciation		135.6	140.2	153.5	153.5
6 Gross profit		1,616.2	1,749.8	1,891.7	2,031.1
7					
8 SG&A		894.7	951.4	1,079.6	1,267.8
9 Amortisation		163.2	175.8	190.3	0.0
10 Operating profit		558.4	622.7	621.7	763.2
11					
12 Non-recurring items		(243.8)	0.0	209.1	0.0
13 Interest Income		3.0	4.9	2.4	
14 Interest Expense		77.3	81.0	71.5	
15 Profit before taxes		727.9	546.6	343.6	763.2
16					
17 Taxes		267.6	212.1	136.4	305.3
18 Net income		460.3	334.5	207.2	457.9
19					
20 Shareholder information					
21 Basic weighted average shares outstanding		140.0	137.3	136.2	136.2
22 Diluted weighted average shares outstanding		141.3	138.4	137.7	137.7
23 Basic earnings per share		$3.29	$2.44	$1.52	$3.36

Diluted earnings per share is derived by taking the earnings available to common shareholders and dividing them by the diluted number of shares outstanding.

DIVIDEND PER SHARE

Dividend per share should be projected using a growth rate in the assumptions area of the model. Simply use a growth formula as shown below:

F25		f_x =E25*(1+Assumptions!F14)				
	B	C	D	E	F	G
A		Hist.	Hist.	Hist.	Proj.	Proj.
1 Irene Foods		31-Dec-99	31-Dec-00	31-Dec-01	31-Dec-02	31-Dec-03
2 Income Statement						
3 Net Sales		3,970.9	4,221.0	4,557.2	4,876.2	5,217.6
4 Clean COGS		2,219.2	2,331.0	2,512.1	2,691.7	2,880.1
5 Depreciation		135.6	140.2	153.5	153.5	155.2
6 Gross profit		1,616.2	1,749.8	1,891.7	2,031.1	2,182.3
7						
8 SG&A		894.7	951.4	1,079.6	1,267.8	1,356.6
9 Amortisation		163.2	175.8	190.3	0.0	0.0
10 Operating profit		558.4	622.7	621.7	763.2	825.7
11						
12 Non-recurring items		(243.8)	0.0	209.1	0.0	0.0
13 Interest Income		3.0	4.9	2.4		
14 Interest Expense		77.3	81.0	71.5		
15 Profit before taxes		727.9	546.6	343.6	763.2	825.7
16						
17 Taxes		267.6	212.1	136.4	305.3	330.3
18 Net income		460.3	334.5	207.2	457.9	495.4
19						
20 Shareholder information						
21 Basic weighted average shares outstanding		140.0	137.3	136.2	136.2	136.2
22 Diluted weighted average shares outstanding		141.3	138.4	137.7	137.7	137.7
23 Basic earnings per share		$3.29	$2.44	$1.52	$3.36	$3.64
24 Diluted earnings per share		$3.26	$2.42	$1.50	$3.33	$3.60
25 Dividend per share		$1.00	$1.06	$1.14	$1.22	$1.30

Projecting the Balance Sheet

Many of the accounts on the balance sheet can be projected as a % of sales. These types of accounts are called sales driven accounts. Other accounts must be derived using BASE analysis derived in the calculations area of the model. Some accounts are projected using an amount in the assumptions area of the model. Finally, the accounts that make the balance sheet balance are excess cash and revolver. The excess cash and revolver line items are addressed in the next section of this reference guide.

SALES-DRIVEN ACCOUNTS

Many of the line items on the balance sheet are projected as a % of sales. These accounts typically include:

- Required / Operating cash
- Trade debtors / Accounts receivable
- Prepaid expenses
- Deferred tax assets / liabilities
- Accrued liabilities
- Other long-term liabilities

Let's take the example of required cash at a growing retail business. As sales increase, the company will need more cash on hand in order to run the business effectively: they need more cash for more cash registers; they need more cash to pay more employees; and so on.

Determining required cash as a % sales is not a precise science, but as a rule of thumb, many practitioners use 3% of sales as a rough guideline. You would enter this % in the assumptions area of the model.

To project sales driven accounts, multiply the % assumption by sales on the income statement. Doing this with the required cash line item is illustrated in the worksheets below.

	A	B	C	D	E	F	G	H
1	Irene Foods		Hist.	Hist.	Hist.	Proj.	Proj.	Proj.
2	Assumptions		31-Dec-99	31-Dec-00	31-Dec-01	31-Dec-02	31-Dec-03	31-Dec-04
16	Required Cash % of sales			0.8%	2.9%	3.0%	3.0%	3.0%

	A	B	C	D	E	F	G
1	Irene Foods		Hist.	Hist.	Hist.	Proj.	Proj.
2	Income Statement		31-Dec-99	31-Dec-00	31-Dec-01	31-Dec-02	31-Dec-03
3	Net Sales		3,970.9	4,221.0	4,557.2	4,876.2	5,217.6
4	Clean COGS		2,219.2	2,331.0	2,512.1	2,691.7	2,880.1

F6	▾	*fx*	=Assumptions!F16*IncState!F3

	A	B	C	D	E	F	G	H
1	Irene Foods		Hist.	Hist.	Hist.	Proj.	Proj.	Proj.
2	Balance Sheet		31-Dec-99	31-Dec-00	31-Dec-01	31-Dec-02	31-Dec-03	31-Dec-04
6	Cash and cash equivalents			32.0	134.1	146.3	156.5	167.5

There are other line items on the balance sheet that are projected as a % of cost of sales (COGS). These typically include:

- Stock/Inventories
- Trade creditors/Accounts payable

To project such accounts, multiply the assumption by the COGS (cost of sales) line item on the income statement. In the worksheets below, projecting inventory is used for illustrative purposes.

	A	B	C	D	E	F	G
1	Irene Foods		Hist.	Hist.	Hist.	Proj.	Proj.
2	Assumptions		31-Dec-99	31-Dec-00	31-Dec-01	31-Dec-02	31-Dec-03
18	Inventories % of COGS			26.0%	20.4%	22.0%	22.0%

	A	B	C	D	E	F	G
1	Irene Foods		Hist.	Hist.	Hist.	Proj.	Proj.
2	Income Statement		31-Dec-99	31-Dec-00	31-Dec-01	31-Dec-02	31-Dec-03
3	Net Sales		3,970.9	4,221.0	4,557.2	4,876.2	5,217.6
4	Clean COGS		2,219.2	2,331.0	2,512.1	2,691.7	2,880.1

F8   ▾   ƒₓ =Assumptions!F18*IncState!F4

	A	B	C	D	E	F	G	H
1	Irene Foods		Hist.	Hist.	Hist.	Proj.	Proj.	Pro
2	Balance Sheet		31-Dec-99	31-Dec-00	31-Dec-01	31-Dec-02	31-Dec-03	31-Dec
6	Cash and cash equivalents			32.0	134.1	146.3	158.5	
7	Accounts receivable			379.7	361.7	390.1	417.4	
8	Inventories			605.2	512.1	592.2	633.6	
9	Deferred income taxes			76.1	96.9	97.5	104.4	

NET FIXED ASSETS (NET PP&E)

The next line item on the balance sheet that your model will need to include is ending net fixed assets (net PP&E). Since you have already calculated this while preparing the income statement (*see Depreciation, page 37*), all you need to do is link the ending net PP&E balance from the calculations section as shown below:

F14   ▾   ƒₓ =Calcs!F7

	A	B	C	D	E	F
1	Irene Foods		Hist.	Hist.	Hist.	Proj.
2	Balance Sheet		31-Dec-99	31-Dec-00	31-Dec-01	31-Dec-02
6	Cash and cash equivalents			32.0	134.1	146.3
7	Accounts receivable			379.7	361.7	390.1
8	Inventories			605.2	512.1	592.2
9	Deferred income taxes			76.1	96.9	97.5
10	Prepaid expenses and other			202.4	62.6	146.3
11	Total current assets			1,295.3	1,167.5	1,510.6
12						
13	*Non-current assets*					
14	Net PP&E			1,585.4	1,534.9	1,552.1

	A	B	C	D	E	F	G	H
1	Irene Foods		Hist.	Hist.	Hist.	Proj.	Proj.	Proj.
2	Calculations		31-Dec-99	31-Dec-00	31-Dec-01	31-Dec-02	31-Dec-03	31-Dec-04
3	PP&E							
4	Net PP&E, beginning balance					1,534.9	1,552.1	1,579.5
5	Capital expenditures		140.8	143.0	170.0	170.7	182.6	195.4
6	Annual depreciation					153.5	155.2	157.9
7	Net PP&E, ending balance				1,534.9	1,552.1	1,579.5	1,616.9

INTANGIBLES

Identifiable intangible assets and goodwill can both be projected by taking the previous year's balance on the balance sheet and deducting the amortization amount provided in the assumptions area of the model.

	A	B	C	D	E	F	G	H
1	Irene Foods		Hist.	Hist.	Hist.	Proj.	Proj.	Proj.
2	Assumptions		31-Dec-99	31-Dec-00	31-Dec-01	31-Dec-02	31-Dec-03	31-Dec-04
8	Amortisation amount		163.2	175.8	190.3	0.0	0.0	0.0

F15	▾	f_x	**=E15-Assumptions!F8**

	A	B	C	D	E	F
1	**Irene Foods**		Hist.	Hist.	Hist.	Proj.
2	**Balance Sheet**		31-Dec-99	31-Dec-00	31-Dec-01	31-Dec-02
6	Cash and cash equivalents			32.0	134.1	146.3
7	Accounts receivable			379.7	361.7	390.1
8	Inventories			605.2	512.1	592.2
9	Deferred income taxes			76.1	96.9	97.5
10	Prepaid expenses and other			202.4	62.6	146.3
11	Total current assets			1,295.3	1,167.5	1,510.6
12						
13	*Non-current assets*					
14	Net PP&E			1,585.4	1,534.9	1,552.1
15	Goodwill			474.4	429.1	429.1

Note: The goodwill amortization expense above is projected as zero as we are assuming that our fictitious company, Irene Foods, reports under US GAAP.

RETAINED EARNINGS

Retained earnings should be calculated using a BASE account in the calculations area of your model. You then link the result into the retained earnings line on the balance sheet. To derive retained earnings, follow these steps:

1. Enter the following line items in the calculations area of your model.

	A	B
1	**Irene Foods**	
2	**Calculations**	
9	**Retained earnings**	
10	Beginning balance	
11	Net income	
12	Dividends paid	
13	Ending balance	

2. Link the retained earnings balance from the last historical year of the balance sheet into the ending retained earnings balance of the retained earnings schedule.

E13	▾	f_x	**=BalSheet!E37**

	A	B	C	D	E	F
1	**Irene Foods**		Hist.	Hist.	Hist.	Proj.
2	**Calculations**		31-Dec-99	31-Dec-00	31-Dec-01	31-Dec-02
9	**Retained earnings**					
10	Beginning balance					
11	Net income					
12	Dividends paid					
13	Ending balance				2,653.2	

3. Link the beginning retained earnings balance of the first projected year to the ending retained earnings balance of the previous year.

F10	▾	f_x	=E13

	A B	C	D	E	F
1	Irene Foods	Hist.	Hist.	Hist.	Proj.
2	Calculations	31-Dec-99	31-Dec-00	31-Dec-01	31-Dec-02
9	**Retained earnings**				
10	Beginning balance				2,653.2
11	Net income				
12	Dividends paid				
13	Ending balance			2,653.2	

4. Link the net income value from the first projected year of the income statement into the first projected year of the retained earnings schedule.

F11	▾	f_x	=IncState!F18

	A B	C	D	E	F
1	Irene Foods	Hist.	Hist.	Hist.	Proj.
2	Calculations	31-Dec-99	31-Dec-00	31-Dec-01	31-Dec-02
9	**Retained earnings**				
10	Beginning balance				2,653.2
11	Net income				457.9
12	Dividends paid				
13	Ending balance			2,653.2	

5. Link the dividends from the first projected year of the income statement into the retained earnings schedule.
   If you derived dividends by growing dividends per share (*see Dividend per share, page 44*), you must link dividends into the retained earnings schedule by multiplying basic dividends per share by basic shares outstanding.

F12	▾	f_x	=IncState!F25*IncState!F21

	A B	C	D	E	F	G	H
1	Irene Foods	Hist.	Hist.	Hist.	Proj.	Proj.	Pr
2	Calculations	31-Dec-99	31-Dec-00	31-Dec-01	31-Dec-02	31-Dec-03	31-D(
9	**Retained earnings**						
10	Beginning balance				2,653.2		
11	Net income				457.9		
12	Dividends paid				165.5		
13	Ending balance			2,653.2			

	A B	C	D	E	F	G
1	Irene Foods	Hist.	Hist.	Hist.	Proj.	Proj.
2	Income Statement	31-Dec-99	31-Dec-00	31-Dec-01	31-Dec-02	31-Dec-03
20	**Shareholder information**					
21	Basic weighted average shares outstanding	140.0	137.3	136.2	136.2	136.2
22	Diluted weighted average shares outstanding	141.3	138.4	137.7	137.7	137.7
23	Basic earnings per share	$3.29	$2.44	$1.52	$3.36	$3.64
24	Diluted earnings per share	$3.26	$2.42	$1.50	$3.33	$3.60
25	Dividend per share	$1.00	$1.06	$1.14	$1.22	$1.30

6. Calculate the ending balance in the retained earnings schedule.

| F13 | | ▾ | f_x | =F10+F11-F12 | |

	A　　B	C	D	E	F
1	Irene Foods	Hist.	Hist.	Hist.	Proj.
2	Calculations	31-Dec-99	31-Dec-00	31-Dec-01	31-Dec-02
9	**Retained earnings**				
10	Beginning balance				2,653.2
11	Net income				457.9
12	Dividends paid				165.5
13	Ending balance			2,653.2	2,945.7

7. Copy each line item in the retained earnings schedule across the worksheet.

	A　　B	C	D	E	F	G	H	I
1	Irene Foods	Hist.	Hist.	Hist.	Proj.	Proj.	Proj.	Proj.
2	Calculations	31-Dec-99	31-Dec-00	31-Dec-01	31-Dec-02	31-Dec-03	31-Dec-04	31-Dec-05
9	**Retained earnings**							
10	Beginning balance				2,653.2	2,945.7	3,264.0	3,609.4
11	Net income				457.9	495.4	535.0	576.8
12	Dividends paid				165.5	177.1	189.5	202.8
13	Ending balance			2,653.2	2,945.7	3,264.0	3,609.4	3,983.4

8. Link the retained earnings ending balance into the balance sheet.

| F37 | | ▾ | f_x | =Calcs!F13 | |

	A　　B	C	D	E	F
1	Irene Foods	Hist.	Hist.	Hist.	Proj.
2	Balance Sheet	31-Dec-99	31-Dec-00	31-Dec-01	31-Dec-02
21	Revolver				0.0
22	Accounts payable		149.2	133.0	148.0
23	Accrued liabilities		358.1	462.9	463.2
24	Accrued income taxes		1.5	2.6	3.1
25	Other short-term debt		257.6	7.0	0.0
26	Total current liabilities		766.4	605.5	614.3
27					
28	*Non-current liabilities*				
29	Total long-term debt		878.2	877.9	877.0
30	Other long-term liabilities		327.7	361.0	385.2
31	Deferred income taxes		300.5	255.8	292.6
32	Total liabilities		2,272.7	2,100.2	2,169.1
33					
34	**Equity**				
35	Common stock		180.0	180.0	180.0
36	Additional paid in capital		13.1	3.3	3.3
37	Retained earnings		2,627.1	2,653.2	2,945.7

TREASURY STOCK

Treasury stock can be calculated by deducting the share repurchases assumption from the previous year's treasury stock balance on the balance sheet.

When a company projects it is going to repurchase some of its stock, enter the share repurchase amount in the assumptions area of the model.

	A	B	C	D	E	F	G
1		Irene Foods	Hist.	Hist.	Hist.	Proj.	Proj.
2		Assumptions	31-Dec-99	31-Dec-00	31-Dec-01	31-Dec-02	31-Dec-03
32		Additional paid in capital			13.1	3.3	3.3
33		Share repurchases $ amount				0.0	0.0

F38	▾	f_x	=E38-Assumptions!F33

	A B	C	D	E	F	
1	Irene Foods		Hist.	Hist.	Hist.	Proj.
2	Balance Sheet		31-Dec-99	31-Dec-00	31-Dec-01	31-Dec-02	3
21	Revolver					0.0
22	Accounts payable			149.2	133.0	148.0
23	Accrued liabilities			358.1	462.9	463.2
24	Accrued income taxes			1.5	2.6	3.1
25	Other short-term debt			257.6	7.0	0.0
26	Total current liabilities			766.4	605.5	614.3
27						
28	Non-current liabilities					
29	Total long-term debt			878.2	877.9	877.0
30	Other long-term liabilities			327.7	361.0	385.2
31	Deferred income taxes			300.5	255.8	292.6
32	Total liabilities			2,272.7	2,100.2	2,169.1
33						
34	Equity					
35	Common stock			180.0	180.0	180.0
36	Additional paid in capital			13.1	3.3	3.3
37	Retained earnings			2,627.1	2,653.2	2,945.7
38	Treasury stock			(1,645.1)	(1,689.2)	(1,689.2)

COMMON STOCK AND ADDITIONAL PAID IN CAPITAL

The Common stock and additional paid in capital accounts (called up share capital and share premium accounts) should be projected by linking them to a constant assumption in the assumptions area of the model. These accounts should be adjusted if you are projecting share issuance or share repurchases.

F35	▾	f_x	=Assumptions!F31

	A B	C	D	E	F
1	Irene Foods		Hist.	Hist.	Proj.
2	Balance Sheet		31-Dec-99	31-Dec-00	31-Dec-01	31-Dec-02
21	Revolver					0.0
22	Accounts payable			149.2	133.0	148.0
23	Accrued liabilities			358.1	462.9	463.2
24	Accrued income taxes			1.5	2.6	3.1
25	Other short-term debt			257.6	7.0	0.0
26	Total current liabilities			766.4	605.5	614.3
27						
28	Non-current liabilities					
29	Total long-term debt			878.2	877.9	877.0
30	Other long-term liabilities			327.7	361.0	385.2
31	Deferred income taxes			300.5	255.8	292.6
32	Total liabilities			2,272.7	2,100.2	2,169.1
33						
34	Equity					
35	Common stock			180.0	180.0	180.0
36	Additional paid in capital			13.1	3.3	3.3

	A B	C	D	E	F	G	H
1	Irene Foods	Hist.	Hist.	Hist.	Proj.	Proj.	Proj.
2	Assumptions	31-Dec-99	31-Dec-00	31-Dec-01	31-Dec-02	31-Dec-03	31-Dec-04
30	Balance sheet: equity						
31	Common stock		180.0	180.0	180.0	180.0	180.0
32	Additional paid in capital		13.1	3.3	3.3	3.3	3.3

SHORT-TERM DEBT

The short-term debt area of the debt schedule should include an area for a revolver and an area for short-term debt. You should set an area up similar to the one below:

	A	B	C	D	E
1	**Irene Foods**		*Hist.*	*Hist.*	*Hist.*
2	**Debt**		*31-Dec-99*	*31-Dec-00*	*31-Dec-01*
3	**Short-term debt**				
4		Revolver balance		0.0	0.0
5					
6		Interest rate			
7		Interest expense			
8					
9		Other short-term debt		257.6	7.0
10					
11		Interest rate			
12		Interest expense			

The revolver balance cannot be projected until the balance sheet is balanced. You should therefore include the line item, but do not include any projected values until later.

As it is not possible to project other short-term debt in the future, the projected short-term debt balances should be set to zero. This zero balance should be included as an assumption in the assumptions area of the model. If there is an additional funding requirement, the revolver will calculate this automatically.

| F9 | | ▾ | | f_x | **=Assumptions!F35** |

	A	B	C	D	E	F	G	H
1	**Irene Foods**		*Hist.*	*Hist.*	*Hist.*	*Proj.*	*Proj.*	*Proj.*
2	**Debt**		*31-Dec-99*	*31-Dec-00*	*31-Dec-01*	*31-Dec-02*	*31-Dec-03*	*31-Dec-04*
9		Other short-term debt			257.6	7.0	0.0	0.0	0.0

	A	B	F	G	H	I	J
1	**Irene Foods**		*Proj.*	*Proj.*	*Proj.*	*Proj.*	*Proj.*
2	**Assumptions**		*31-Dec-02*	*31-Dec-03*	*31-Dec-04*	*31-Dec-05*	*31-Dec-06*
34	*Debt*						
35		Other short-term debt balance	0.0	0.0	0.0	0.0	0.0

LONG-TERM DEBT

The long-term debt area of the model should appear on the debt schedule under the short-term debt area. A typical long-term debt area will look as follows:

	A	B	C	D	E	F	G	H
			Hist.	Hist.	Hist.	Proj.	Proj.	Proj.
1	Irene Foods		31-Dec-99	31-Dec-00	31-Dec-01	31-Dec-02	31-Dec-03	31-Dec-04
2	Debt							
14	Long-term debt							
15	6.7% Notes due 2005							
16	Beginning balance					200.0	200.0	200.0
17	Repayment					0.0	0.0	0.0
18	Ending balance			200.0	200.0	200.0	200.0	200.0
19								
20	Interest rate					6.70%	6.70%	6.70%
21	Interest expense							
22								
23	6.95% Notes due 2007							
24	Beginning balance					150.0	150.0	150.0
25	Repayment					0.0	0.0	0.0
26	Ending balance			150.0	150.0	150.0	150.0	150.0
27								
28	Interest rate					6.95%	6.95%	6.95%
29	Interest expense					10.4	10.4	10.4
30								
31	6.95% Notes due 2012							
32	Beginning balance					150.0	150.0	150.0
33	Repayment					0.0	0.0	0.0
34	Ending balance			150.0	150.0	150.0	150.0	150.0
35								
36	Interest rate					6.95%	6.95%	6.95%
37	Interest expense					10.4	10.4	10.4
38								
39	8.8% Debentures due 2021							
40	Beginning balance					100.0	100.0	100.0
41	Repayment					0.0	0.0	0.0
42	Ending balance			100.0	100.0	100.0	100.0	100.0
43								
44	Interest rate					8.80%	8.80%	8.80%
45	Interest expense					8.8	8.8	8.8

Each line of long-term debt will have its own mini schedule. To set up a mini schedule, follow these steps:

1. Create the line items shown in rows 15 – 21 of the worksheet below. Then enter the historical ending debt balances for each particular line of long-term debt.

	A	B	C	D	E
			Hist.	Hist.	Hist.
1	Irene Foods		31-Dec-99	31-Dec-00	31-Dec-01
2	Debt				
14	Long-term debt				
15	6.7% Notes due 2005				
16	Beginning balance				
17	Repayment				
18	Ending balance			200.0	200.0
19					
20	Interest rate				
21	Interest expense				

2. Link the beginning debt balance of the first projected year to the ending debt balance of the previous year.

F16			f_x	=E18	

	A	B	C	D	E	F
			Hist.	Hist.	Hist.	Proj.
1	Irene Foods		31-Dec-99	31-Dec-00	31-Dec-01	31-Dec-02
2	Debt					
14	Long-term debt					
15	6.7% Notes due 2005					
16	Beginning balance					200.0
17	Repayment					
18	Ending balance			200.0	200.0	
19						
20	Interest rate					
21	Interest expense					

3. Now set up a repayment schedule in the assumptions area of the model for each line of debt. In the example shown below, the debt is repaid in one lump sum in 2005. This is known as a bullet repayment.

	A	B	F	G	H	I	J
1	Irene Foods		Proj.	Proj.	Proj.	Proj.	Proj.
2	Assumptions		31-Dec-02	31-Dec-03	31-Dec-04	31-Dec-05	31-Dec-06
36	6.7% Notes due 2005 repayment		0.0	0.0	0.0	200.0	0.0

4. Link the repayment for the first projected year to the relevant repayment in the assumptions area.

F17   *fx* **=Assumptions!F36**

	A	B	C	D	E	F	G
1	Irene Foods		Hist.	Hist.	Hist.	Proj.	Proj.
2	Debt		31-Dec-99	31-Dec-00	31-Dec-01	31-Dec-02	31-Dec-03
14	**Long-term debt**						
15	6.7% Notes due 2005						
16	Beginning balance					200.0	
17	Repayment					0.0	
18	Ending balance			200.0	200.0		

5. Calculate the ending debt balance for the first projected year.

F18   *fx* **=F16-F17**

	A	B	C	D	E	F
1	Irene Foods		Hist.	Hist.	Hist.	Proj.
2	Debt		31-Dec-99	31-Dec-00	31-Dec-01	31-Dec-02
14	**Long-term debt**					
15	6.7% Notes due 2005					
16	Beginning balance					200.0
17	Repayment					0.0
18	Ending balance			200.0	200.0	200.0

6. Copy the three line items in the first projected year across to complete the schedule.

	A	B	C	D	E	F	G	H	I	J
1	Irene Foods		Hist.	Hist.	Hist.	Proj.	Proj.	Proj.	Proj.	Proj.
2	Debt		31-Dec-99	31-Dec-00	31-Dec-01	31-Dec-02	31-Dec-03	31-Dec-04	31-Dec-05	31-Dec-06
14	**Long-term debt**									
16	6.7% Notes due 2005									
16	Beginning balance					200.0	200.0	200.0	200.0	0.0
17	Repayment					0.0	0.0	0.0	200.0	0.0
18	Ending balance			200.0	200.0	200.0	200.0	200.0	0.0	0.0

7. Set up an interest rate assumption in the assumptions area of your model. The description of this debt indicates that the interest rate is 6.7%. We can add this to the assumptions area as shown below:

	A	B	F	G	H	I	J
1	Irene Foods		Proj.	Proj.	Proj.	Proj.	Proj.
2	Assumptions		31-Dec-02	31-Dec-03	31-Dec-04	31-Dec-05	31-Dec-06
42	**Interest**						
43	Revolver		5.00%	5.00%	5.00%	5.00%	5.00%
44	Other short-term debt		5.00%	5.00%	5.00%	5.00%	5.00%
45	6.7% Notes due 2005		6.70%	6.70%	6.70%	6.70%	6.70%

8. Link the interest rate into the interest line on the debt schedule and copy it across.

F20   *fx* **=Assumptions!F45**

	A	B	C	D	E	F	G	H
1	Irene Foods		Hist.	Hist.	Hist.	Proj.	Proj.	Proj.
2	Debt		31-Dec-99	31-Dec-00	31-Dec-01	31-Dec-02	31-Dec-03	31-Dec-04
14	**Long-term debt**							
15	6.7% Notes due 2005							
16	Beginning balance					200.0	200.0	200.0
17	Repayment					0.0	0.0	0.0
18	Ending balance			200.0	200.0	200.0	200.0	200.0
20	Interest rate					6.70%	6.70%	6.70%

You don't need to calculate interest expense at this stage. Subsequent sections of this reference guide will explain how

Once you have included all lines of debt in your debt schedule, you should set up a debt summary area under the long-term debt area of the debt schedule. To set up a debt summary area, follow these steps:

1. Enter the following line items under the long-term area of the debt schedule.

63	Debt Summary
64	Revolver
65	Other short-term debt
66	Long-term debt
67	Total Debt

2. Link the revolver balance line into the debt summary and copy across. You should do this, even though the revolver line item is empty.

	A	B	C	D	E	F	G	H
1	Irene Foods		Hist.	Hist.	Hist.	Proj.	Proj.	Pro
2	Debt		31-Dec-99	31-Dec-00	31-Dec-01	31-Dec-02	31-Dec-03	31-De
63	Debt Summary							
64	Revolver			0.0	0.0	0.0	0.0	

3. Link the other short-term debt balance line into the debt summary and copy across.

D65   ▾ f_x **=D9**

	A	B	C	D	E	F	G	H
1	Irene Foods		Hist.	Hist.	Hist.	Proj.	Proj.	Pro
2	Debt		31-Dec-99	31-Dec-00	31-Dec-01	31-Dec-02	31-Dec-03	31-De
63	Debt Summary							
64	Revolver			0.0	0.0	0.0	0.0	
65	Other short-term debt			257.6	7.0	0.0	0.0	

4. Add up the individual long-term debt balance lines in the debt summary and copy across.

D66   ▾ f_x **=SUM(D18,D26,D34,D42,D50,D58)**

	A	B	C	D	E	F	G	H	I	J
1	Irene Foods		Hist.	Hist.	Hist.	Proj.	Proj.	Proj.	Proj.	Proj.
2	Debt		31-Dec-99	31-Dec-00	31-Dec-01	31-Dec-02	31-Dec-03	31-Dec-04	31-Dec-05	31-Dec-06
63	Debt Summary									
64	Revolver			0.0	0.0	0.0	0.0	0.0	0.0	0.0
65	Other short-term debt			257.6	7.0	0.0	0.0	0.0	0.0	0.0
66	Long-term debt			878.2	877.9	877.0	859.9	859.9	657.7	657.6

5. Calculate total debt in the total line and copy across.

D67   ▾ f_x **=SUM(D64:D66)**

	A	B	C	D	E	F	G
1	Irene Foods		Hist.	Hist.	Hist.	Proj.	Proj.	F
2	Debt		31-Dec-99	31-Dec-00	31-Dec-01	31-Dec-02	31-Dec-03	31-(
63	Debt Summary						
64	Revolver			0.0	0.0	0.0	0.0
65	Other short-term debt			257.6	7.0	0.0	0.0
66	Long-term debt			878.2	877.9	877.0	859.9
67	Total Debt			1,135.8	884.9	877.0	859.9

Now that you have set up a debt summary, you should link the short term and long-term debt line items to the balance sheet. Do not link the revolver at this stage!

F25   ⚬   *fx*   =Debt!F9

	B	C	D	E	F	G	H
1	Irene Foods	Hist.	Hist.	Hist.	Proj.	Proj.	Proj.
2	Balance Sheet	31-Dec-99	31-Dec-00	31-Dec-01	31-Dec-02	31-Dec-03	31-Dec-0
21	Revolver				0.0	0.0	
22	Accounts payable		149.2	133.0	148.0	158.4	1
23	Accrued liabilities		358.1	462.9	463.2	495.7	5
24	Accrued income taxes		1.5	2.6	3.1	3.3	
25	Other short-term debt		257.6	7.0	0.0	0.0	

F29   ⚬   *fx*   =Debt!F66

	B	C	D	E	F	G	H
1	Irene Foods	Hist.	Hist.	Hist.	Proj.	Proj.	Proj.
2	Balance Sheet	31-Dec-99	31-Dec-00	31-Dec-01	31-Dec-02	31-Dec-03	31-Dec-
21	Revolver				0.0	0.0	
22	Accounts payable		149.2	133.0	148.0	158.4	
23	Accrued liabilities		358.1	462.9	463.2	495.7	5
24	Accrued income taxes		1.5	2.6	3.1	3.3	
25	Other short-term debt		257.6	7.0	0.0	0.0	
26	Total current liabilities		766.4	605.5	614.3	657.4	
27							
28	Non-current liabilities						
29	Total long-term debt		878.2	877.9	877.0	859.9	8

You will notice that the historical debt balances are also linked to the debt schedule. This is not the case with the other balance sheet accounts.

Balancing the Balance Sheet

BALANCE CHECK

You should add a balance check line under the balance sheet before attempting to balance the model. This line will contain an IF statement that either returns the text "OK" if the balance sheet balances or returns the difference if the balance sheet does not balance. To add the balance check, follow these steps:

1. Enter the Balance Check line item under the balance sheet as shown below.

	A	B	C
1	**Irene Foods**		*Hist.*
2	**Balance Sheet**		*31-Dec-99*
36	Additional paid in capital		
37	Retained earnings		
38	Treasury stock		
39	Total equity		
40	*Total liabilities & equity*		
41			
42	*Balance Check*		

2. Enter an IF statement in the first historical year that checks to see if the balance sheet balances.

D42	▾	ƒx	=IF(D17=D40,"OK",D17-D40)

	A	B	C	D	E	F	G	H
1	Irene Foods		*Hist.*	*Hist.*	*Hist.*	*Proj.*	*Proj.*	*Pro*
2	Balance Sheet		*31-Dec-99*	*31-Dec-00*	*31-Dec-01*	*31-Dec-02*	*31-Dec-03*	*31-De*
36	Additional paid in capital			13.1	3.3	3.3	3.3	
37	Retained earnings			2,627.1	2,653.2	2,945.7	3,264.0	3
38	Treasury stock			(1,645.1)	(1,689.2)	(1,689.2)	(1,689.2)	(1
39	Total equity			1,175.0	1,147.2	1,439.7	1,758.0	2
40	*Total liabilities & equity*			3,447.8	3,247.4	3,608.8	4,000.5	4
41								
42	*Balance Check*			OK				

In the example above, cell D17 contains the total assets value and cell D40 contains the total liabilities and equity figure. In this case, the balance sheet is in US format. A similar IF statement could be used for a UK style net assets balance sheet. Such an IF statement would simply test whether Net Assets = Equity.

3. Copy the IF statement across and make sure that the balance sheet balances in the historical years. If it does not, the balance sheet will never balance in the projected years.

	A	B	C	D	E	F	G	H
1	Irene Foods		*Hist.*	*Hist.*	*Hist.*	*Proj.*	*Proj.*	*Proj.*
2	Balance Sheet		*31-Dec-99*	*31-Dec-00*	*31-Dec-01*	*31-Dec-02*	*31-Dec-03*	*31-Dec-04*
35	Common stock			180.0	180.0	180.0	180.0	180.0
36	Additional paid in capital			13.1	3.3	3.3	3.3	3.3
37	Retained earnings			2,627.1	2,653.2	2,945.7	3,264.0	3,609.4
38	Treasury stock			(1,645.1)	(1,689.2)	(1,689.2)	(1,689.2)	(1,689.2)
39	Total equity			1,175.0	1,147.2	1,439.7	1,758.0	2,103.4
40	*Total liabilities & equity*			3,447.8	3,247.4	3,608.8	4,000.5	4,442.7
41								
42	*Balance Check*			OK	OK	(138.2)	(398.2)	(691.4)

As you can see, the projected years of the balance sheet do not balance yet. This will be addressed by building the cash flow statement.

Don't Worry!

Your balance sheet is not meant to balance at this stage.

CASH FLOW STATEMENT

The cash flow statement is the key to balancing the balancing sheet. It is always a reconciliation of the effect on cash of the difference between the beginning and ending balance sheet. A cash flow used for US reporting purposes contains 4 key areas:

Cash Flow from Operating Activities: Cash flow from operating activities are those which arise as a result of day-to-day operating activities, such as making sales, purchasing supplies, paying bills to suppliers and paying salaries. It defines the cash available to make necessary investments and to satisfy the interest and dividend obligations of the business.

Cash Flow from Investing Activities: Cash flow from investing activities are those which arise as a result of investments in the future growth of the business. Capital expenditure and investments in stocks and bonds of other companies are examples of investing cash flows.

Cash Flow from Financing: Cash flow from financing includes any cash flows relating to financing the business through debt and equity. Paying dividends, repaying debt, issuing debt and raising cash through issuing equity are all examples of financing cash flows.

Net Cash Flow: Net cash flow is the sum of cash flows from operations, cash flows from investing and cash flows from financing. It is added to the previous year's cash on the balance sheet to arrive at the ending cash balance for the current year after all operating, investing and financing decisions for the year have been accounted for.

FOUR RULES OF CASH

There four rules of cash. These are as follows:

Rules		Example
Assets ↑	Cash ↓	Capital expenditure would increase assets and result in a cash outflow.
Assets ↓	Cash ↑	A customer paying an outstanding invoice would cause receivables or debtors to decrease and would increase cash.
L&E ↑	Cash ↑	Issuing debt or equity would cause liabilities and equity to increase and cash to increase.
L&E ↓	Cash ↓	Paying back debt or repurchasing shares would cause liabilities and equity to decrease and cash to decrease.

MARK-UP THE BALANCE SHEET

Before building the cash flow statement, you should mark up the
balance sheet to help you easily identify which type of cash flow each
balance sheet account is associated with. To do this, place an "O",
"I" or "F" next to every single balance sheet account depending on
whether the account in question will give rise to an operating cash
flow, an investing cash flow or a financing cash flow, respectively.
As you build the cash flow relating to each account on the balance
sheet, you will gradually remove the marks. This will ensure that
you don't overlook any accounts when building the cash flow, which
would cause the balance sheet not to balance. In the balance sheet
below, these marks have been input in column K.

	B	F	G	H	I	J	K
1	Irene Foods	Proj.	Proj.	Proj.	Proj.	Proj.	
2	Balance Sheet	31-Dec-02	31-Dec-03	31-Dec-04	31-Dec-05	31-Dec-06	
3	**Assets**						
4	*Current assets*						
5	Excess Cash						
6	Cash and cash equivalents	146.3	156.5	167.5	179.2	191.8	
7	Accounts receivable	390.1	417.4	446.6	477.9	511.3	o
8	Inventories	592.2	633.6	678.0	725.4	776.2	o
9	Deferred income taxes	97.5	104.4	111.7	119.5	127.8	o
10	Prepaid expenses and other	146.3	156.5	167.5	179.2	191.8	o
11	Total current assets	1,372.4	1,468.4	1,571.2	1,681.2	1,798.9	
12							
13	*Non-current assets*						
14	Net PP&E	1,552.1	1,579.5	1,616.9	1,664.3	1,721.6	io
15	Goodwill	429.1	429.1	429.1	429.1	429.1	o
16	Other assets	117.0	125.2	134.0	143.4	153.4	i
17	Total assets	3,470.6	3,602.3	3,751.3	3,918.0	4,103.0	
18							
19	**Liabilities**						
20	*Current liabilities*						
21	Revolver	0.0	0.0	0.0	0.0	0.0	
22	Accounts payable	148.0	158.4	169.5	181.4	194.1	o
23	Accrued liabilities	463.2	495.7	530.4	567.5	607.2	o
24	Accrued income taxes	3.1	3.3	3.6	3.8	4.1	o
25	Other short-term debt	0.0	0.0	0.0	0.0	0.0	f
26	Total current liabilities	614.3	657.4	703.4	752.7	805.4	
27							
28	*Non-current liabilities*						
29	Total long-term debt	877.0	859.9	859.8	657.7	657.6	f
30	Other long-term liabilities	385.2	412.2	441.0	471.9	504.9	o
31	Deferred income taxes	292.6	313.1	335.0	358.4	383.5	o
32	Total liabilities	2,169.1	2,242.5	2,339.2	2,240.7	2,351.5	
33							
34	**Equity**						
35	Common stock	180.0	180.0	180.0	180.0	180.0	f
36	Additional paid in capital	3.3	3.3	3.3	3.3	3.3	f
37	Retained earnings	2,945.7	3,264.0	3,609.4	3,983.4	4,387.6	f
38	Treasury stock	(1,689.2)	(1,689.2)	(1,689.2)	(1,689.2)	(1,689.2)	f
39	Total equity	1,439.7	1,758.0	2,103.4	2,477.5	2,881.6	
40	Total liabilities & equity	3,608.8	4,000.5	4,442.7	4,718.2	5,233.1	

Some balance sheet accounts will have two marks next to them,
since they give rise to changes in two areas of cash flow. Net PP&E,
for example, is marked with an O and an I since it affects both the
operating cash flow and the investing cash flow. Another example
is retained earnings, which affects both operating cash flows and
financing cash flows.

Net PP&E: Net PP&E is derived using a BASE account in the
calculations area of the model. Two components cause this change:
capital expenditure and depreciation. Capital expenditure is an
investing cash flow while depreciation affects the operating cash flow.

	B	F	G	H	I	J
1	Irene Foods	Proj.	Proj.	Proj.	Proj.	Proj.
2	Calculations	31-Dec-02	31-Dec-03	31-Dec-04	31-Dec-05	31-Dec-06
3	PP&E					
4	Net PP&E, beginning balance	1,534.9	1,552.1	1,579.5	1,616.9	1,664.3
5	Capital expenditures	170.7	182.6	195.4	209.1	223.7
6	Annual depreciation	153.5	155.2	157.9	161.7	166.4
7	Net PP&E, ending balance	1,552.1	1,579.5	1,616.9	1,664.3	1,721.6

Retained Earnings: The retained earnings account is also derived using a BASE analysis in the calculations area of the model. There are two components that cause Retained Earnings to change. These are: Net income and Dividends. Net income goes in the operating section of the cash flow and dividends in the financing section of the cash flow.

	A B	F	G	H	I	J
1	Irene Foods	Proj.	Proj.	Proj.	Proj.	Proj.
2	Calculations	31-Dec-02	31-Dec-03	31-Dec-04	31-Dec-05	31-Dec-06
9	**Retained earnings**					
10	Beginning balance	2,653.2	2,945.7	3,264.0	3,609.4	3,983.4
11	Net income	457.9	495.4	535.0	576.8	621.1
12	Dividends paid	165.5	177.1	189.5	202.8	217.0
13	Ending balance	2,945.7	3,264.0	3,609.4	3,983.4	4,387.6

MODELING CASH FLOW FROM OPERATIONSX

Net Income

When modeling cash flow from operations, the first line item on your cash flow should be Net income. This should be linked to the income statement. You can now remove the "O" mark from the retained earnings line item on the balance sheet.

F4		f_x	=IncState!F18		

	A B	F	G	H	I	J
1	**Irene Foods**	Proj.	Proj.	Proj.	Proj.	Proj.
2	**Cash Flow**	31-Dec-02	31-Dec-03	31-Dec-04	31-Dec-05	31-Dec-06
3	**Cash flow from operations**					
4	Net income	457.9	495.4	535.0	576.8	621.1

Non-Cash Items

Non-cash items should be added back, such as deprecation and amortization. Both depreciation and amortization can be linked in from the income statement. Now remove the "O" mark from PP&E and the "O" mark from intangibles.

F5		f_x	=IncState!F5		

	A B	F	G	H	I	J
1	**Irene Foods**	Proj.	Proj.	Proj.	Proj.	Proj.
2	**Cash Flow**	31-Dec-02	31-Dec-03	31-Dec-04	31-Dec-05	31-Dec-06
3	**Cash flow from operations**					
4	Net income	457.9	495.4	535.0	576.8	621.1
5	Depreciation	153.5	155.2	157.9	161.7	166.4

F6		f_x	=IncState!F9		

	A B	F	G	H	I	J
1	**Irene Foods**	Proj.	Proj.	Proj.	Proj.	Proj.
2	**Cash Flow**	31-Dec-02	31-Dec-03	31-Dec-04	31-Dec-05	31-Dec-06
3	**Cash flow from operations**					
4	Net income	457.9	495.4	535.0	576.8	621.1
5	Depreciation	153.5	155.2	157.9	161.7	166.4
6	Amortisation	0.0	0.0	0.0	0.0	0.0

OPERATING WORKING CAPITAL

Now you must include the cash effect of changes in operating working capital. Rather than having separate line items on the cash flow for all the operating working capital accounts, it is common practice to calculate operating working capital in the calculations area of the model. To calculate operating working capital:

1. Enter the operating working capital line items in the calculations area of the model.

	A	B
1	**Irene Foods**	
2	**Calculations**	
15	**Operating working capital**	
16	Accounts receivable	
17	Inventories	
18	Deferred income taxes	
19	Prepaid expenses and other	
20	**Total operating assets**	
21	Accounts payable	
22	Accrued liabilities	
23	Accrued income taxes	
24	**Total operating liabilities**	
25		
26	**Operating Working Capital**	

2. Link the operating asset accounts to the balance sheet.

F16			f_x	=BalSheet!F7		
	A	B	F	G	H	I	J
1	Irene Foods		Proj.	Proj.	Proj.	Proj.	Proj.
2	Calculations		31-Dec-02	31-Dec-03	31-Dec-04	31-Dec-05	31-Dec-06
15	Operating working capital						
16	Accounts receivable		390.1	417.4	446.6	477.9	511.3
17	Inventories		592.2	633.6	678.0	725.4	776.2
18	Deferred income taxes		97.5	104.4	111.7	119.5	127.8
19	Prepaid expenses and other		146.3	156.5	167.5	179.2	191.8

3. Calculate total operating assets.

F20			f_x	=SUM(F16:F19)		
	A	B	F	G	H	I	J
1	Irene Foods		Proj.	Proj.	Proj.	Proj.	Proj.
2	Calculations		31-Dec-02	31-Dec-03	31-Dec-04	31-Dec-05	31-Dec-06
15	Operating working capital						
16	Accounts receivable		390.1	417.4	446.6	477.9	511.3
17	Inventories		592.2	633.6	678.0	725.4	776.2
18	Deferred income taxes		97.5	104.4	111.7	119.5	127.8
19	Prepaid expenses and other		146.3	156.5	167.5	179.2	191.8
20	**Total operating assets**		1,226.1	1,311.9	1,403.7	1,502.0	1,607.1

> **Time saving tip!**
>
> Rather than typing the individual operating working capital headings, you can link them to the balance sheet. As long as your model has matrix integrity, you can then copy these across and down and the appropriate operating working capital numbers will appear.

4. Link the operating liabilities to the balance sheet.

F21		f_x =BalSheet!F22				
		F	**G**	**H**	**I**	**J**
A	**B**					
1	Irene Foods	Proj.	Proj.	Proj.	Proj.	Proj.
2	Calculations	31-Dec-02	31-Dec-03	31-Dec-04	31-Dec-05	31-Dec-06
15	**Operating working capital**					
16	Accounts receivable	390.1	417.4	446.6	477.9	511.3
17	Inventories	592.2	633.6	678.0	725.4	776.2
18	Deferred income taxes	97.5	104.4	111.7	119.5	127.8
19	Prepaid expenses and other	146.3	156.5	167.5	179.2	191.8
20	**Total operating assets**	**1,226.1**	**1,311.9**	**1,403.7**	**1,502.0**	**1,607.1**
21	Accounts payable	148.0	158.4	169.5	181.4	194.1
22	Accrued liabilities	463.2	495.7	530.4	567.5	607.2
23	Accrued income taxes	3.1	3.3	3.6	3.8	4.1

5. Calculate total operating liabilities.

F24		f_x =SUM(F21:F23)				
		F	**G**	**H**	**I**	**J**
A	**B**					
1	Irene Foods	Proj.	Proj.	Proj.	Proj.	Proj.
2	Calculations	31-Dec-02	31-Dec-03	31-Dec-04	31-Dec-05	31-Dec-06
15	**Operating working capital**					
16	Accounts receivable	390.1	417.4	446.6	477.9	511.3
17	Inventories	592.2	633.6	678.0	725.4	776.2
18	Deferred income taxes	97.5	104.4	111.7	119.5	127.8
19	Prepaid expenses and other	146.3	156.5	167.5	179.2	191.8
20	**Total operating assets**	1,226.1	1,311.9	1,403.7	1,502.0	1,607.1
21	Accounts payable	148.0	158.4	169.5	181.4	194.1
22	Accrued liabilities	463.2	495.7	530.4	567.5	607.2
23	Accrued income taxes	3.1	3.3	3.6	3.8	4.1
24	**Total operating liabilities**	**614.3**	**657.4**	**703.4**	**752.7**	**805.4**

6. Calculate operating working capital by deducting operating liabilities from operating assets.

F26		f_x =F20-F24				
		F	**G**	**H**	**I**	**J**
A	**B**					
1	Irene Foods	Proj.	Proj.	Proj.	Proj.	Proj.
2	Calculations	31-Dec-02	31-Dec-03	31-Dec-04	31-Dec-05	31-Dec-06
15	**Operating working capital**					
16	Accounts receivable	390.1	417.4	446.6	477.9	511.3
17	Inventories	592.2	633.6	678.0	725.4	776.2
18	Deferred income taxes	97.5	104.4	111.7	119.5	127.8
19	Prepaid expenses and other	146.3	156.5	167.5	179.2	191.8
20	**Total operating assets**	1,226.1	1,311.9	1,403.7	1,502.0	1,607.1
21	Accounts payable	148.0	158.4	169.5	181.4	194.1
22	Accrued liabilities	463.2	495.7	530.4	567.5	607.2
23	Accrued income taxes	3.1	3.3	3.6	3.8	4.1
24	**Total operating liabilities**	614.3	657.4	703.4	752.7	805.4
25						
26	**Operating Working Capital**	**611.7**	**654.5**	**700.3**	**749.3**	**801.7**

> **The Δ symbol**
>
> **To add the change symbol (Δ) to your cash flow statement, type the letter D and change the font of the character to Symbol. Make sure you select the individual D character within the cell before applying the Symbol font style.**

Now that you have calculated operating working capital, you must calculate the change in operating working capital in the cash flow statement:

F7		f_x =Calcs!E26-Calcs!F26				
		F	**G**	**H**	**I**	**J**
A	**B**					
1	Irene Foods	Proj.	Proj.	Proj.	Proj.	Proj.
2	Cash Flow	31-Dec-02	31-Dec-03	31-Dec-04	31-Dec-05	31-Dec-06
3	**Cash flow from operations**					
4	Net income	457.9	495.4	535.0	576.8	621.1
5	Depreciation	153.5	155.2	157.9	161.7	166.4
6	Amortisation	0.0	0.0	0.0	0.0	0.0
7	Δ Operating working capital	(176.9)	(42.8)	(45.8)	(49.0)	(52.4)

In order to calculate operating working capital, you must take last year's operating working capital balance minus this year's operating working capital balance in order to achieve the correct signage in the cash flow. In the example above, as operating working capital increases from 2001 to 2002, cash will decrease in 2002.

Now you can remove the "O" marks from all the operating working capital line items on the balance sheet!

OTHER OPERATING ACCOUNTS

You must include in the cash flow statement any other accounts that would give rise to operating cash flows. In the example used in this document there are two such accounts: Deferred tax liabilities and other long-term liabilities.

F8		f_x	=BalSheet!F30-BalSheet!E30

	A	B	F	G	H	I	J	K
1	**Irene Foods**		Proj.	Proj.	Proj.	Proj.	Proj.	
2	**Cash Flow**		31-Dec-02	31-Dec-03	31-Dec-04	31-Dec-05	31-Dec-06	
3	**Cash flow from operations**							
4	Net income		457.9	495.4	535.0	576.8	621.1	
5	Depreciation		153.5	155.2	157.9	161.7	166.4	
6	Amortisation		0.0	0.0	0.0	0.0	0.0	
7	Δ Operating working capital		(176.9)	(42.8)	(45.8)	(49.0)	(52.4)	
8	Δ Other long-term liabilities		24.2	27.0	28.9	30.9	33.0	

F9		f_x	=BalSheet!F31-BalSheet!E31

	A	B	F	G	H	I	J	K
1	**Irene Foods**		Proj.	Proj.	Proj.	Proj.	Proj.	
2	**Cash Flow**		31-Dec-02	31-Dec-03	31-Dec-04	31-Dec-05	31-Dec-06	
3	**Cash flow from operations**							
4	Net income		457.9	495.4	535.0	576.8	621.1	
5	Depreciation		153.5	155.2	157.9	161.7	166.4	
6	Amortisation		0.0	0.0	0.0	0.0	0.0	
7	Δ Operating working capital		(176.9)	(42.8)	(45.8)	(49.0)	(52.4)	
8	Δ Other long-term liabilities		24.2	27.0	28.9	30.9	33.0	
9	Δ Deferred tax liabilities		36.8	20.5	21.9	23.4	25.1	

As both of these accounts are liabilities, to calculate the cash flow you must deduct this year's account balance from last year's account balance. For example, as deferred taxes increase from 255.7 to 292.5, the resulting cash flow is 36.8 as shown above. Once again, you can now remove the "O" marks.

NET CASH FLOW FROM OPERATIONS

To calculate net cash flow from operations, simply add up the operating cash flows as shown below:

F10		f_x	=SUM(F4:F9)

	A	B	F	G	H	
1	**Irene Foods**		Proj.	Proj.	Proj.	
2	**Cash Flow**		31-Dec-02	31-Dec-03	31-Dec-04	31
3	**Cash flow from operations**					
4	Net income		457.9	495.4	535.0	
5	Depreciation		153.5	155.2	157.9	
6	Amortisation		0.0	0.0	0.0	
7	Δ Operating working capital		(176.9)	(42.8)	(45.8)	
8	Δ Other long-term liabilities		24.2	27.0	28.9	
9	Δ Deferred tax liabilities		36.8	20.5	21.9	
10	**Total cash from operations**		495.6	655.3	697.9	

> **Quick sum!**
>
> **To quickly SUM operating cash flow, select the cell to contain the SUM formula (in this case, cell F10) then hold down ALT and press the equals [=] key. Check the SUM range and press ENTER.**

CASH FLOW FROM INVESTING

The cash flow from investing area of the cash flow should include all cash flows resulting from investing activities. These normally include:

- Capital expenditure
- Purchase of intangibles
- Change in other long-term assets
- Proceeds from sale of fixed assets

Capital expenditure and other long-term assets are used in the model illustrated in this document.

Capital expenditure is an investing cash flow. It should be linked to the calculations area of the model and should be a negative number as it represents a cash outflow. To ensure capital expenditure appears as a negative number, add a minus sign before the formula.

F13   ▾ f_x =-Calcs!F5

	B	F	G	H	I	J
1	**Irene Foods**	Proj.	Proj.	Proj.	Proj.	Proj.
2	**Cash Flow**	*31-Dec-02*	*31-Dec-03*	*31-Dec-04*	*31-Dec-05*	*31-Dec-06*
3	**Cash flow from operations**					
4	Net income	457.9	495.4	535.0	576.8	621.1
5	Depreciation	153.5	155.2	157.9	161.7	166.4
6	Amortisation	0.0	0.0	0.0	0.0	0.0
7	Δ Operating working capital	(176.9)	(42.8)	(45.8)	(49.0)	(52.4)
8	Δ Other long-term liabilities	24.2	27.0	28.9	30.9	33.0
9	Δ Deferred tax liabilities	36.8	20.5	21.9	23.4	25.1
10	**Total cash from operations**	**495.6**	**655.3**	**697.9**	**743.8**	**793.3**
11						
12	**Cash flow from investing**					
13	Capital expenditure	(170.7)	(182.6)	(195.4)	(209.1)	(223.7)

Other long-term assets are normally an investing cash flow, which we will assume for this example. To derive the cash flow from other long-term assets, the formula should be last year's balance minus this year's balance as shown below:

F14   ▾ f_x =BalSheet!E16-BalSheet!F16

	B	F	G	H	I	J	K
1	**Irene Foods**	Proj.	Proj.	Proj.	Proj.	Proj.	
2	**Cash Flow**	*31-Dec-02*	*31-Dec-03*	*31-Dec-04*	*31-Dec-05*	*31-Dec-06*	
3	**Cash flow from operations**						
4	Net income	457.9	495.4	535.0	576.8	621.1	
5	Depreciation	153.5	155.2	157.9	161.7	166.4	
6	Amortisation	0.0	0.0	0.0	0.0	0.0	
7	Δ Operating working capital	(176.9)	(42.8)	(45.8)	(49.0)	(52.4)	
8	Δ Other long-term liabilities	24.2	27.0	28.9	30.9	33.0	
9	Δ Deferred tax liabilities	36.8	20.5	21.9	23.4	25.1	
10	**Total cash from operations**	**495.6**	**655.3**	**697.9**	**743.8**	**793.3**	
11							
12	**Cash flow from investing**						
13	Capital expenditure	(170.7)	(182.6)	(195.4)	(209.1)	(223.7)	
14	Δ Other assets	(1.2)	(8.2)	(8.8)	(9.4)	(10.0)	

Once you have included all the investing cash flow accounts, calculate total cash flow from investing as shown below:

F15			fx	=SUM(F13:F14)		
	A	B	F	G	H	I
1	Irene Foods		Proj.	Proj.	Proj.	Proj.
2	Cash Flow		31-Dec-02	31-Dec-03	31-Dec-04	31-Dec-05
3	Cash flow from operations					
4	Net income		457.9	495.4	535.0	576.8
5	Depreciation		153.5	155.2	157.9	161.7
6	Amortisation		0.0	0.0	0.0	0.0
7	Δ Operating working capital		(176.9)	(42.8)	(45.8)	(49.0)
8	Δ Other long-term liabilities		24.2	27.0	28.9	30.9
9	Δ Deferred tax liabilities		36.8	20.5	21.9	23.4
10	Total cash from operations		495.6	655.3	697.9	743.8
11						
12	Cash flow from investing					
13	Capital expenditure		(170.7)	(182.6)	(195.4)	(209.1)
14	Δ Other assets		(1.2)	(8.2)	(8.8)	(9.4)
15	Total cash from investing		(171.8)	(190.8)	(204.2)	(218.5)

Remember to remove the "I" marks from the investing cash flow accounts.

CASH FLOW FROM FINANCING

The cash flow from financing section should include all those cash flows resulting from the financing of the business. These normally include:

- Issuance or repayment of debt
- Issuance or repurchase of equity
- Dividends

To derive the cash flows from financing activities, simply calculate the change in the relevant balance sheet accounts, removing the "F" marks as you do them.

	A	B	F	G	H	I	J
1	Irene Foods		Proj.	Proj.	Proj.	Proj.	Proj.
2	Cash Flow		31-Dec-02	31-Dec-03	31-Dec-04	31-Dec-05	31-Dec-06
15	Total cash from investing		(171.8)	(190.8)	(204.2)	(218.5)	(233.7)
16							
17	Cash flow from financing						
18	Increase (decrease) in other STD		(7.0)	0.0	0.0	0.0	0.0
19	Increase (decrease) in LTD		(0.9)	(17.1)	(0.1)	(202.1)	(0.1)
20	Increase (decrease) in Common stock		0.0	0.0	0.0	0.0	0.0
21	Increase (decrease) in APIC		0.0	0.0	0.0	0.0	0.0
22	Share repurchases		0.0	0.0	0.0	0.0	0.0
23	Dividends		(165.5)	(177.1)	(189.5)	(202.8)	(217.0)

Let's take other short-term debt as an example. In the model illustrated in this reference guide, short-term debt decreases from $7m in 2001 to $0 in 2002. This gives rise to a cash outflow of $7m as debt is being repaid. Therefore the formula to calculate cash flow arising from short-term debt is:

F18			fx	=BalSheet!F25-BalSheet!E25			
	A	B	F	G	H	I	J	K
1	Irene Foods		Proj.	Proj.	Proj.	Proj.	Proj.	
2	Cash Flow		31-Dec-02	31-Dec-03	31-Dec-04	31-Dec-05	31-Dec-06	
18	Increase (decrease) in other STD		(7.0)	0.0	0.0	0.0	0.0	
19	Increase (decrease) in LTD		(0.9)	(17.1)	(0.1)	(202.1)	(0.1)	
20	Increase (decrease) in Common stock		0.0	0.0	0.0	0.0	0.0	
21	Increase (decrease) in APIC		0.0	0.0	0.0	0.0	0.0	
22	Share repurchases		0.0	0.0	0.0	0.0	0.0	

Share repurchases should be linked to the assumptions area and should be a negative number as they represent a cash outflow.

F22	▾	f_x	=-Assumptions!F33		
	B	**F**	**G**	**H**	**I**	**J**
1	Irene Foods	Proj.	Proj.	Proj.	Proj.	Proj.
2	Cash Flow	31-Dec-02	31-Dec-03	31-Dec-04	31-Dec-05	31-Dec-06
18	Increase (decrease) in other STD	(7.0)	0.0	0.0	0.0	0.0
19	Increase (decrease) in LTD	(0.9)	(17.1)	(0.1)	(202.1)	(0.1)
20	Increase (decrease) in Common stock	0.0	0.0	0.0	0.0	0.0
21	Increase (decrease) in APIC	0.0	0.0	0.0	0.0	0.0
22	Share repurchases	0.0	0.0	0.0	0.0	0.0

Dividends should be linked to the retained earnings BASE analysis in the calculations area of the model. They should be a negative number as they represent a cash outflow.

F23	▾	f_x	=-Calcs!F12	
	B	**F**	**G**	**H**	**I**
1	Irene Foods	Proj.	Proj.	Proj.	Proj.
2	Cash Flow	31-Dec-02	31-Dec-03	31-Dec-04	31-Dec-
18	Increase (decrease) in other STD	(7.0)	0.0	0.0	(
19	Increase (decrease) in LTD	(0.9)	(17.1)	(0.1)	(20.
20	Increase (decrease) in Common stock	0.0	0.0	0.0	(
21	Increase (decrease) in APIC	0.0	0.0	0.0	(
22	Share repurchases	0.0	0.0	0.0	(
23	Dividends	(165.5)	(177.1)	(189.5)	(20.

Once you have included all the financing cash flows, calculate total cash flows from financing as follows:

F24	▾	f_x	=SUM(F18:F23)	
	B	**F**	**G**	**H**	**I**
1	Irene Foods	Proj.	Proj.	Proj.	Proj.
2	Cash Flow	31-Dec-02	31-Dec-03	31-Dec-04	31-Dec-0:
17	**Cash flow from financing**				
18	Increase (decrease) in other STD	(7.0)	0.0	0.0	0.(
19	Increase (decrease) in LTD	(0.9)	(17.1)	(0.1)	(202.
20	Increase (decrease) in Common stock	0.0	0.0	0.0	0.(
21	Increase (decrease) in APIC	0.0	0.0	0.0	0.(
22	Share repurchases	0.0	0.0	0.0	0.(
23	Dividends	(165.5)	(177.1)	(189.5)	(202.8
24	**Total cash from financing**	(173.4)	(194.2)	(189.6)	(404.9

NET CASH FLOW

Net cash flow is the sum of cash flow from operations, cash flow from investing, and cash flow from financing.

F26		fx	=SUM(F10,F15,F24)		

	B	F	G	H	I
1	**Irene Foods**	Proj.	Proj.	Proj.	Proj.
2	**Cash Flow**	31-Dec-02	31-Dec-03	31-Dec-04	31-Dec-05 31
3	**Cash flow from operations**				
4	Net income	457.9	495.4	535.0	576.8
5	Depreciation	153.5	155.2	157.9	161.7
6	Amortisation	0.0	0.0	0.0	0.0
7	Δ Operating working capital	(176.9)	(42.8)	(45.8)	(49.0)
8	Δ Other long-term liabilities	24.2	27.0	28.9	30.9
9	Δ Deferred tax liabilities	36.8	20.5	21.9	23.4
10	**Total cash from operations**	**495.6**	**655.3**	**697.9**	**743.8**
11					
12	**Cash flow from investing**				
13	Capital expenditure	(170.7)	(182.6)	(195.4)	(209.1)
14	Δ Other assets	(1.2)	(8.2)	(8.8)	(9.4)
15	**Total cash from investing**	**(171.8)**	**(190.8)**	**(204.2)**	**(218.5)**
16					
17	**Cash flow from financing**				
18	Increase (decrease) in other STD	(7.0)	0.0	0.0	0.0
19	Increase (decrease) in LTD	(0.9)	(17.1)	(0.1)	(202.1)
20	Increase (decrease) in Common stock	0.0	0.0	0.0	0.0
21	Increase (decrease) in APIC	0.0	0.0	0.0	0.0
22	Share repurchases	0.0	0.0	0.0	0.0
23	Dividends	(165.5)	(177.1)	(189.5)	(202.8)
24	**Total cash from financing**	**(173.4)**	**(194.2)**	**(189.6)**	**(404.9)**
25					
26	**Net cash flow**	**150.3**	**270.3**	**304.1**	**120.5**

EXCESS CASH / REVOLVER

Sometimes the company you are modeling will generate more cash than it requires. Your model should allow for this by including an Excess cash account. If the company does not generate enough cash and requires additional funding, your model can address this through a Revolver account. The excess cash account and the revolver account provide essential information about the financing requirements of the business. They are also key to making the balance sheet balance.

The excess cash line item should be added to the current assets section of the balance sheet. When doing this, make sure that you adjust your total current assets SUM function otherwise the balance sheet will not balance!

	B	F	G	H	I	J
1	**Irene Foods**	Proj.	Proj.	Proj.	Proj.	Proj.
2	**Balance Sheet**	31-Dec-02	31-Dec-03	31-Dec-04	31-Dec-05	31-Dec-06
3	**Assets**					
4	*Current assets*					
5	Excess cash					

The revolver should be added to the current liabilities section of the balance sheet. Once again, when doing this, make sure you adjust the total current liabilities SUM function to include the revolver in total liabilities.

F21		fx			

	B	F	G	H	I	J
1	**Irene Foods**	Proj.	Proj.	Proj.	Proj.	Proj.
2	**Balance Sheet**	31-Dec-02	31-Dec-03	31-Dec-04	31-Dec-05	31-Dec-06
18						
19	**Liabilities**					
20	*Current liabilities*					
21	Revolver					

CALCULATING EXCESS CASH/REVOLVER

To calculate whether the company generates excess cash or has an additional funding requirement (revolver), follow these steps:

1. Input the following line items under the cash flow.

	A	B
1	**Irene Foods**	
2	**Cash Flow**	
28	*Excess Cash / Revolver*	
29		Beginning cash
30		Change in cash from CFS
31		Net cash available at end of year
32		
33		Required cash
34		Excess cash / (Revolver)

2. Link the "Net cash available at end of year" line item for the latest historical year to the cash balance on the balance sheet as shown below.

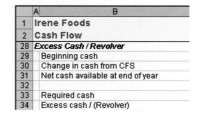

E31	f_x =BalSheet!E6

	B	C	D	E	
1	Irene Foods	*Hist.*	*Hist.*	*Hist.*	
2	Cash Flow	*31-Dec-99*	*31-Dec-00*	*31-Dec-01*	*31*
28	*Excess Cash / Revolver*				
29	Beginning cash				
30	Change in cash from CFS				
31	Net cash available at end of year			134.1	
32					
33	Required cash				
34	Excess cash / (Revolver)				

3. Link the beginning cash balance of the first projected year to the "Net cash available at end of year" of the previous year.

F29	f_x =E31

	B	C	D	E	F	G
1	Irene Foods	*Hist.*	*Hist.*	*Hist.*	*Proj.*	*Proj.*
2	Cash Flow	*31-Dec-99*	*31-Dec-00*	*31-Dec-01*	*31-Dec-02*	*31-Dec-03*
28	*Excess Cash / Revolver*					
29	Beginning cash				134.1	
30	Change in cash from CFS					
31	Net cash available at end of year			134.1		
32						
33	Required cash					
34	Excess cash / (Revolver)					

4. Link the "Change in cash from CFS" line item to the Net cash flow from the cash flow statement.

F30		f_x	=F26

	A	B	C	D	E	F
1	Irene Foods		Hist.	Hist.	Hist.	Proj.
2	Cash Flow		31-Dec-99	31-Dec-00	31-Dec-01	31-Dec-02
25						
26	Net cash flow					150.3
27						
28	*Excess Cash / Revolver*					
29	Beginning cash					134.1
30	Change in cash from CFS					150.3
31	Net cash available at end of year				134.1	
32						
33	Required cash					
34	Excess cash / (Revolver)					

5. Calculate "net cash available at end of year" by adding the "beginning cash" and "change in cash from CFS" together.

F31		f_x	=F29+F30

	A	B	C	D	E	F
1	Irene Foods		Hist.	Hist.	Hist.	Proj.
2	Cash Flow		31-Dec-99	31-Dec-00	31-Dec-01	31-Dec-02
25						
26	Net cash flow					150.3
27						
28	*Excess Cash / Revolver*					
29	Beginning cash					134.1
30	Change in cash from CFS					150.3
31	Net cash available at end of year				134.1	284.5
32						
33	Required cash					
34	Excess cash / (Revolver)					

6. Next, link the "required cash" to the required cash line item on the balance sheet.

F33		f_x	=BalSheet!F6

	A	B	C	D	E	F
1	Irene Foods		Hist.	Hist.	Hist.	Proj.
2	Cash Flow		31-Dec-99	31-Dec-00	31-Dec-01	31-Dec-02
25						
26	Net cash flow					150.3
27						
28	*Excess Cash / Revolver*					
29	Beginning cash					134.1
30	Change in cash from CFS					150.3
31	Net cash available at end of year				134.1	284.5
32						
33	Required cash					146.3
34	Excess cash / (Revolver)					

	A	B	F	G	H	I	J
1	Irene Foods		Proj.	Proj.	Proj.	Proj.	Proj.
2	Balance Sheet		31-Dec-02	31-Dec-03	31-Dec-04	31-Dec-05	31-Dec-06
3	Assets						
4	Current assets						
5	Excess cash						
6	Required cash		146.3	156.5	167.5	179.2	191.8

7.   To calculate "excess cash / (revolver)", deduct "required cash" from "net cash available at the end of year".

	A	B	C	D	E	F
1	Irene Foods		Hist.	Hist.	Hist.	Proj.
2	Cash Flow		31-Dec-99	31-Dec-00	31-Dec-01	31-Dec-02
25						
26	Net cash flow					150.3
27						
28	Excess Cash / Revolver					
29	Beginning cash					134.1
30	Change in cash from CFS					150.3
31	Net cash available at end of year				134.1	284.5
32						
33	Required cash					146.3
34	Excess cash / (Revolver)					138.2

A positive number means that the business has generated more cash than it needs. This number will therefore go on the excess cash line of the balance sheet. A negative number means that the business requires additional funding. This number will therefore go on the revolver line of the balance sheet.

8.   Copy the entire cash flow column across. In the worksheet above, you should copy column F across the remaining projected years.

	A	B	C	D	E	F	G	H	I
1	Irene Foods		Hist.	Hist.	Hist.	Proj.	Proj.	Proj.	Proj.
2	Cash Flow		31-Dec-99	31-Dec-00	31-Dec-01	31-Dec-02	31-Dec-03	31-Dec-04	31-Dec-05
25									
26	Net cash flow					150.3	270.3	304.1	120.5
27									
28	Excess Cash / Revolver								
29	Beginning cash					134.1	284.5	554.7	858.9
30	Change in cash from CFS					150.3	270.3	304.1	120.5
31	Net cash available at end of year				134.1	284.5	554.7	858.9	979.4
32									
33	Required cash					146.3	156.5	167.5	179.2
34	Excess cash / (Revolver)					138.2	398.2	691.4	800.1

Once you have completed your cash flow as described above, the excess cash / (revolver) number should equal the Balance Check line on the balance sheet.

Balance Sheet Extract

37	Retained earnings	2,653.2	2,945.7	3,264.0	3,609.4	3,983.4	4,387.5
38	Treasury stock	(1,689.2)	(1,689.2)	(1,689.2)	(1,689.2)	(1,689.2)	(1,689.2)
39	Total equity	1,147.2	1,439.7	1,758.0	2,103.4	2,477.5	2,881.6
40	Total Liab.& Equity	3,247.4	3,608.8	4,000.5	4,442.7	4,718.2	5,233.1
41							
42	Balance Check	OK	(138.2)	(398.2)	(691.4)	(800.1)	(1,130.0)

Cash Flow Statement extract

28	Excess Cash / Revolver					
29	Beginning cash		134.1	284.5	554.7	858.9	979.4
30	Change in cash from CFS		150.3	270.3	304.1	120.5	342.4
31	Net cash available at end of year	134.1	284.5	554.7	858.9	979.4	1,321.8
32							
33	Required Cash		146.3	156.5	167.5	179.2	191.8
34	Excess Cash / (Revolver)		138.2	398.2	691.4	800.1	1,130.0

BALANCING THE BALANCE SHEET

As already mentioned, the excess cash / (revolver) line on the cash flow statement provides the key to making the balance sheet balance. A positive number on this line represents excess cash and must be linked into the excess cash line on the balance sheet. A negative number on this line represent a revolver and should be linked into the revolver line on the balance sheet. The most effective way to achieve this is by using Excel's MAX and MIN functions.

The MAX function returns the highest number in a range and the MIN function returns the lowest number in a range. This is illustrated below:

A6			▾		f_x	**=MAX(A1:A5)**	
	A	B	C	D	E	F	G
1	3						
2	-56						
3	90						
4	-78						
5	89						
6	90						

A6			▾		f_x	**=MIN(A1:A5)**	
	A	B	C	D	E	F	G
1	3						
2	-56						
3	90						
4	-78						
5	89						
6	-78						

The excess cash line on the balance sheet should contain a MAX function that has the **excess cash/(revolver)** number on the cash flow and **zero** as its arguments. The MAX function will return the higher of these two numbers. Therefore, if the excess cash / (revolver) number on the cash flow is positive, the MAX function will return this positive number as it is higher than zero. However, if the excess cash / (revolver) number on the cash flow is negative, the MAX function will return zero since zero is higher than the negative number.

F5			▾		f_x	=MAX(0,Cash!F34)	
A	B	F	G	H	I	J
1 Irene Foods		Proj.	Proj.	Proj.	Proj.	Proj.
2 Balance Sheet		31-Dec-02	31-Dec-03	31-Dec-04	31-Dec-05	31-Dec-06
3 Assets						
4 Current assets						
5 Excess cash		138.2	398.2	691.4	800.1	1,130.0

Likewise, the revolver line on the balance sheet should contain a MIN function that has the excess cash / (revolver) number on the cash flow and zero as its arguments. The MIN function will return the lower of these two numbers. Therefore, if the excess cash / (revolver) number is negative, the MIN function will return this negative number. If the excess cash / (revolver) number is positive, the MIN function will return zero as zero is the lower of the two numbers. As the MIN function will return the revolver as a negative number on the balance sheet, you must insert a minus sign before the function as shown below.

F21			f_x	**=-MIN(Cash!F34,0)**

	A B	F	G	H	I	J
1	Irene Foods	Proj.	Proj.	Proj.	Proj.	Proj.
2	Balance Sheet	31-Dec-82	31-Dec-83	31-Dec-84	31-Dec-85	31-Dec-86
19	**Liabilities**					
20	*Current liabilities*					
21	Revolver	0.0	0.0	0.0	0.0	0.0

Now your balance sheet should balance!

	A B	F	G	H	I	J
1	**Irene Foods**	Proj.	Proj.	Proj.	Proj.	Proj.
2	**Balance Sheet**	31-Dec-82	31-Dec-83	31-Dec-84	31-Dec-85	31-Dec-86
3	**Assets**					
4	*Current assets*					
5	Excess cash	138.2	398.2	691.4	800.1	1,130.0
6	Required cash	146.3	156.5	167.5	179.2	191.8
7	Accounts receivable	390.1	417.4	446.5	477.9	511.3
8	Inventories	592.2	633.6	678.0	725.4	776.2
9	Deferred income taxes	97.5	104.4	111.7	119.5	127.8
10	Prepaid expenses and other	146.3	156.5	167.5	179.2	191.8
11	Total current assets	1,510.6	1,866.6	2,262.6	2,481.4	2,928.9
12						
13	*Non-current assets*					
14	Net PP&E	1,552.1	1,579.5	1,616.9	1,664.3	1,721.6
15	Goodwill	429.1	429.1	429.1	429.1	429.1
16	Other assets	117.0	125.2	134.0	143.4	153.4
17	*Total assets*	3,608.8	4,000.5	4,442.7	4,718.2	5,233.1
18						
19	**Liabilities**					
20	*Current liabilities*					
21	Revolver	0.0	0.0	0.0	0.0	0.0
22	Accounts payable	148.0	158.4	169.5	181.4	194.1
23	Accrued liabilities	463.2	495.7	530.4	567.5	607.2
24	Accrued income taxes	3.1	3.3	3.6	3.8	4.1
25	Other short-term debt	0.0	0.0	0.0	0.0	0.0
26	Total current liabilities	614.3	657.4	703.4	752.7	805.4
27						
28	*Non-current liabilities*					
29	Total long-term debt	877.0	859.9	859.8	657.7	657.6
30	Other long-term liabilities	385.2	412.2	441.0	471.9	504.9
31	Deferred income taxes	292.6	313.1	335.0	358.4	383.5
32	Total liabilities	2,169.1	2,242.5	2,339.2	2,240.7	2,351.5
33						
34	**Equity**					
35	Common stock	180.0	180.0	180.0	180.0	180.0
36	Additional paid in capital	3.3	3.3	3.3	3.3	3.3
37	Retained earnings	2,945.7	3,264.0	3,609.4	3,983.4	4,387.6
38	Treasury stock	(1,689.2)	(1,689.2)	(1,689.2)	(1,689.2)	(1,689.2)
39	Total equity	1,439.7	1,758.0	2,103.4	2,477.5	2,881.6
40	*Total liabilities & equity*	3,608.8	4,000.5	4,442.7	4,718.2	5,233.1
41						
42	*Balance Check*	OK	OK	OK	OK	OK

ADDING THE REVOLVER LINE TO THE DEBT SCHEDULE

Once the balance sheet balances, you must link the revolver line on the balance sheet to the revolver area of the debt schedule as shown below.

F4			f_x	**=BalSheet!F21**

	A B	F	G	H	I	J
1	Irene Foods	Proj.	Proj.	Proj.	Proj.	Proj.
2	Debt	31-Dec-82	31-Dec-83	31-Dec-84	31-Dec-85	31-Dec-86
3	**Short-term debt**					
4	Revolver balance	0.0	0.0	0.0	0.0	0.0
5						
6	Interest rate	5.00%	5.00%	5.00%	5.00%	5.00%
7	Interest expense	0.0	0.0	0.0	0.0	0.0

Interest Income and Interest Expense

The final step in creating a fully integrated model is adding interest income and interest expense to the income statement.

METHODS OF INTEREST CALCULATION

There are two ways to calculate interest income and expense in a model. These are:

- Multiply last year's debt or cash balance by the interest rate.
- Multiple the average of last year's and this year's debt or cash balances by the interest rate.

Both methods have their advantages and disadvantages. These are outlined below:

INACCURATE INTEREST CALCULATIONS

Using last year's debt balance instead of an average of last year and this year's debt balance often lead to inaccurate interest calculations. This is especially the case if the debt or cash balance varies a lot from year to year. The following example will help to explain this:

Debby's Debt

Debby's debt balance as at 31st December 2001 was $100. On March 31st 2002, she repaid $75 of this debt. Her debt balance as at 31st December 2002 was therefore $25. The interest rate on her debt is 10%.

If we calculate Debby's interest using last year's debt, we get $10 ($100 * 10%). If we calculate Debby's interest using this year's debt we get $2.50 ($25 * 10%). If we calculate Debby's interest using an average of last year's and this year's debt we get $6.30 ((100+25)/2 *10%).

If we use last year's debt balance, our interest calculation is too high. If we were to use this year's debt balance, our interest calculation would be too low. An average of the two debt balances, while not 100% accurate, gives us a much better representation of the amount of interest expense. The same applies to cash balances and interest income.

CIRCULARITY

Using an average debt or cash balance in a model makes the model circular.

The diagram below indicates why the model is circular. Interest feeds into net income on the income statement, then net income feeds into the cash flow; cash flow in turn determines the cash / debt balance for the year; and finally the cash / debt balances determine the interest income or expense. In other words, interest determines the excess cash / revolver balance, while the excess cash / revolver balance also determines interest.

Circularity in Excel can be problematic if not handled correctly. Therefore, some people prefer to use last year's debt balance as this method of interest calculation does not cause circularity. The logic here is that even though this method can lead to inaccurate interest calculations, given the likely errors in predicting sales and other variables, the additional error caused by a failure to determine interest income or expense accurately is usually not that important!

CALCULATING INTEREST EXPENSE

Interest expense can be calculated on the debt schedule area of your model. Included in the debt line items should be a line item for the interest rate and a line item for the interest expense.

	A B	F Proj.	G Proj.	H Proj.	I Proj.	J Proj.
1	Irene Foods	Proj.	Proj.	Proj.	Proj.	Proj.
2	Debt	31-Dec-02	31-Dec-03	31-Dec-04	31-Dec-05	31-Dec-06
14	Long-term debt					
15	6.7% Notes due 2005					
16	Beginning balance	200.0	200.0	200.0	200.0	0.0
17	Repayment	0.0	0.0	0.0	200.0	0.0
18	Ending balance	200.0	200.0	200.0	0.0	0.0
19						
20	Interest rate					
21	Interest expense					

INTEREST RATES

The assumptions page should contain the interest rates used by the model, and they should be linked into each interest rate line in the debt schedule. An example of this is shown below:

	A B	F Proj. 31-Dec-02	G Proj. 31-Dec-03	H Proj. 31-Dec-04	I Proj. 31-Dec-05	J Proj. 31-Dec-06
1	Irene Foods					
2	Assumptions					
42	**Interest**					
43	Revolver	5.00%	5.00%	5.00%	5.00%	5.00%
44	Other short-term debt	5.00%	5.00%	5.00%	5.00%	5.00%
45	6.7% Notes due 2005	6.70%	6.70%	6.70%	6.70%	6.70%
46	6.95% Notes due 2007	6.95%	6.95%	6.95%	6.95%	6.95%
47	6.95% Notes due 2012	6.95%	6.95%	6.95%	6.95%	6.95%
48	8.8% Debentures due 2021	8.80%	8.80%	8.80%	8.80%	8.80%
49	7.2% Debentures due 2027	7.20%	7.20%	7.20%	7.20%	7.20%
50	Other long-term debt repayment	5.00%	5.00%	5.00%	5.00%	5.00%
51	Cash	3.00%	3.00%	3.00%	3.00%	3.00%

F20   ▾   _fx_   **=Assumptions!F45**

	A B	F Proj. 31-Dec-02	G Proj. 31-Dec-03	H Proj. 31-Dec-04	I Proj. 31-Dec-05	J Proj. 31-Dec-06
1	Irene Foods					
2	Debt					
14	**Long-term debt**					
15	_6.7% Notes due 2005_					
16	Beginning balance	200.0	200.0	200.0	200.0	0.0
17	Repayment	0.0	0.0	0.0	200.0	0.0
18	Ending balance	200.0	200.0	200.0	0.0	0.0
19						
20	Interest rate	6.70%	6.70%	6.70%	6.70%	6.70%

INTEREST EXPENSE

To calculate interest expense for a particular line of debt, either multiply last year's ending debt balance by the interest rate or multiply the average of last year and this year by the interest rate, depending on your chosen method. Both methods are shown below:

Last Year Method:

F21   ▾   _fx_   **=E18*F20**

	A B	E Hist. 31-Dec-01	F Proj. 31-Dec-02	G Proj. 31-Dec-03	H Proj. 31-Dec-04	I Proj. 31-Dec-05	J Proj. 31-Dec-06
1	Irene Foods						
2	Debt						
14	**Long-term debt**						
15	_6.7% Notes due 2005_						
16	Beginning balance		200.0	200.0	200.0	200.0	0.0
17	Repayment		0.0	0.0	0.0	200.0	0.0
18	Ending balance	200.0	200.0	200.0	200.0	0.0	0.0
19							
20	Interest rate		6.70%	6.70%	6.70%	6.70%	6.70%
21	Interest expense		13.4	13.4	13.4	13.4	0.0

Average Method:

F21   ▾   _fx_   **=AVERAGE(E18:F18)*F20**

	A B	E Hist. 31-Dec-01	F Proj. 31-Dec-02	G Proj. 31-Dec-03	H Proj. 31-Dec-04	I Proj. 31-Dec-05	J Proj. 31-Dec-06
1	Irene Foods						
2	Debt						
14	**Long-term debt**						
15	_6.7% Notes due 2005_						
16	Beginning balance		200.0	200.0	200.0	200.0	0.0
17	Repayment		0.0	0.0	0.0	200.0	0.0
18	Ending balance	200.0	200.0	200.0	200.0	0.0	0.0
19							
20	Interest rate		6.70%	6.70%	6.70%	6.70%	6.70%
21	Interest expense		13.4	13.4	13.4	6.7	0.0

You will notice that the two methods yield the same figures for interest expense until 2005. When debt balances remain constant, there is no interest expense impact between using the last year or average method.

INTEREST EXPENSE SUMMARY

Once you have calculated interest for all the debt lines as described above, you must create an interest expense summary area below the debt schedule. This summary simply adds together the interest expense of all the different debt lines.

		F	G	H	I	J
		Proj.	Proj.	Proj.	Proj.	Proj.
1	Irene Foods					
2	Debt	31-Dec-02	31-Dec-03	31-Dec-04	31-Dec-05	31-Dec-06
69	**Interest expense summary**					
70	Short-term debt interest	0.2	0.0	0.0	0.0	0.0
71	Long-term debt interest	62.4	62.0	61.5	54.8	48.0
72	**Total Interest Expense**	62.6	62.0	61.5	54.8	48.0

CALCULATING INTEREST INCOME

Interest income is normally calculated in the debt area of the model. To calculate interest income:

1. Create the following line items under the debt area.

	A	B
1		**Irene Foods**
2		**Debt**
74		**Interest Income**
75		Excess cash
76		Required cash
77		Total cash
78		
79		Interest rate
80		Interest income

2. Link excess cash and required cash to the excess cash and required cash line items on the balance sheet. When doing this, make sure that you include one year of historical numbers.

F75			fx	=BalSheet!F5

		F	G	H	I	J
		Proj.	Proj.	Proj.	Proj.	Proj.
1	Irene Foods					
2	Debt	31-Dec-02	31-Dec-03	31-Dec-04	31-Dec-05	31-Dec-06
74	**Interest Income**					
75	Excess cash	138.2	398.2	691.4	800.1	1,130.0

		F	G	H	I	J
		Proj.	Proj.	Proj.	Proj.	Proj.
1	Irene Foods					
2	Debt	31-Dec-02	31-Dec-03	31-Dec-04	31-Dec-05	31-Dec-06
74	**Interest Income**					
75	Excess cash	138.2	398.2	691.4	800.1	1,130.0
76	Required cash	146.3	156.5	167.5	179.2	191.8

3. Calculate total cash.

F77			fx	=SUM(F75:F76)

		F	G	H	I	J
		Proj.	Proj.	Proj.	Proj.	Proj.
1	Irene Foods					
2	Debt	31-Dec-02	31-Dec-03	31-Dec-04	31-Dec-05	31-Dec-06
74	**Interest Income**					
75	Excess cash	138.2	398.2	691.4	800.1	1,130.0
76	Required cash	146.3	156.5	167.5	179.2	191.8
77	Total cash	284.5	554.7	858.9	979.4	1,321.8

4. Link the interest rate to the cash interest rate in the assumptions area.

| F79 | ▼ | *fx* | =Assumptions!F51 |

	B	F	G	H	I	J
1	Irene Foods	Proj.	Proj.	Proj.	Proj.	Proj.
2	Debt	31-Dec-82	31-Dec-83	31-Dec-84	31-Dec-85	31-Dec-86
74	Interest Income					
75	Excess cash	138.2	398.2	691.4	800.1	1,130.0
76	Required cash	146.3	156.5	167.5	179.2	191.8
77	Total cash	284.5	554.7	858.9	979.4	1,321.8
78						
79	Interest rate	3.00%	3.00%	3.00%	3.00%	3.00%

	B	F	G	H	I	J
1	Irene Foods	Proj.	Proj.	Proj.	Proj.	Proj.
2	Assumptions	31-Dec-82	31-Dec-83	31-Dec-84	31-Dec-85	31-Dec-86
51	Cash	3.00%	3.00%	3.00%	3.00%	3.00%

5. Calculate interest income using the last year method or using the average method.

Last Year

| F80 | ▼ | *fx* | =E77*F79 |

	B	E	F	G	H	I	J
1	Irene Foods	Hist.	Proj.	Proj.	Proj.	Proj.	Proj.
2	Debt	31-Dec-81	31-Dec-82	31-Dec-83	31-Dec-84	31-Dec-85	31-Dec-86
74	Interest Income						
75	Excess cash	0.0	138.2	398.2	691.4	800.1	1,130.0
76	Required cash	134.1	146.3	156.5	167.5	179.2	191.8
77	Total cash	134.1	284.5	554.7	858.9	979.4	1,321.8
78							
79	Interest rate		3.00%	3.00%	3.00%	3.00%	3.00%
80	Interest income		4.0	8.5	16.6	25.8	29.4

Average

| F80 | ▼ | *fx* | =AVERAGE(E77:F77)*F79 |

	B	E	F	G	H	I	J
1	Irene Foods	Hist.	Proj.	Proj.	Proj.	Proj.	Proj.
2	Debt	31-Dec-81	31-Dec-82	31-Dec-83	31-Dec-84	31-Dec-85	31-Dec-86
74	Interest Income						
75	Excess cash	0.0	138.2	398.2	691.4	800.1	1,130.0
76	Required cash	134.1	146.3	156.5	167.5	179.2	191.8
77	Total cash	134.1	284.5	554.7	858.9	979.4	1,321.8
78							
79	Interest rate		3.00%	3.00%	3.00%	3.00%	3.00%
80	Interest income		6.3	12.6	21.2	27.6	34.5

LINKING INTEREST INTO THE INCOME STATEMENT

Now you are at the final stage of creating your model: feeding the interest expense and interest income into the income statement.

LAST YEAR METHOD

If you calculated interest expense and interest income using the last year method, you can simply link the interest items into the income statement and the model is complete!

	F13	▾				f_x	=Debt!F80	
	A	B		F	G	H	I	J
1	Irene Foods			Proj.	Proj.	Proj.	Proj.	Proj.
2	Income Statement			31-Dec-02	31-Dec-03	31-Dec-04	31-Dec-05	31-Dec-06
3	Net Sales			4,876.2	5,217.6	5,582.8	5,973.6	6,391.8
4	Clean COGS			2,691.7	2,880.1	3,081.7	3,297.4	3,528.3
5	Depreciation			153.5	155.2	157.9	161.7	166.4
6	**Gross profit**			**2,031.1**	**2,182.3**	**2,343.2**	**2,514.5**	**2,697.1**
7								
8	SG&A			1,267.8	1,356.6	1,451.5	1,553.1	1,661.9
9	Amortisation			0.0	0.0	0.0	0.0	0.0
10	**Operating profit**			**763.2**	**825.7**	**891.6**	**961.3**	**1,035.2**
11								
12	Non-recurring items			0.0	0.0	0.0	0.0	0.0
13	Interest Income			5.8	11.1	18.9	24.6	31.1
14	Interest Expense			62.6	62.0	61.5	54.8	48.0
15	**Profit before taxes**			**706.4**	**774.8**	**849.0**	**931.1**	**1,018.3**
16								
17	Taxes			282.6	309.9	339.6	372.5	407.3
18	**Net income**			**423.8**	**464.9**	**509.4**	**558.7**	**611.0**

AVERAGE METHOD

If you calculated interest using the average method, as soon as you link one of the interest items into the model, the following error message will appear:

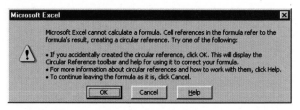

This is telling you that the formula you are about to create is circular and Excel does not automatically calculate formulae that are circular! Choose cancel to clear the dialog box. You will notice that the interest is now set at zero.

In order for Excel to calculate interest income and expense, the iteration settings must be activated. To do this:

1.   Choose Tool, Options from them menu. The following dialog box is displayed.

2.   Choose the Calculation tab.

3.   Activate the Iteration check box.

4.   Choose OK.

Once you have done this, you can add both interest items to the income statement.

F13		f_x	=Debt!F80		
	F	**G**	**H**	**I**	**J**
A B	Proj.	Proj.	Proj.	Proj.	Proj.
1 Irene Foods					
2 Income Statement	31-Dec-02	31-Dec-03	31-Dec-04	31-Dec-05	31-Dec-06
3 Net Sales	4,876.2	5,217.6	5,582.8	5,973.6	6,391.8
4 Clean COGS	2,691.7	2,880.1	3,081.7	3,297.4	3,528.3
5 Depreciation	153.5	155.2	157.9	161.7	166.4
6 **Gross profit**	**2,031.1**	**2,182.3**	**2,343.2**	**2,514.5**	**2,697.1**
7					
8 SG&A	1,267.8	1,356.6	1,451.5	1,553.1	1,661.9
9 Amortisation	0.0	0.0	0.0	0.0	0.0
10 **Operating profit**	**763.2**	**825.7**	**891.6**	**961.3**	**1,035.2**
11					
12 Non-recurring items	0.0	0.0	0.0	0.0	0.0
13 Interest Income	5.8	11.1	18.9	24.6	31.1
14 Interest Expense	62.6	62.0	61.5	54.8	48.0
15 **Profit before taxes**	**706.4**	**774.8**	**849.0**	**931.1**	**1,018.3**
16					
17 Taxes	282.6	309.9	339.6	372.5	407.3
18 **Net income**	**423.8**	**464.9**	**509.4**	**558.7**	**611.0**

A PROBLEM WITH CIRCULAR MODELS

One of the main reasons why people do not like working with circular models is that they are easy to "blow up"! In other words, such models can become infected with error values such as #REF or #VALUE, which appear to be impossible to resolve. Circular models get into this state for a number of reasons. Accidentally deleting a row that a formula is dependent on is one reason. Accidentally typing text into a cell that a formula is dependent on is another reason. Even if you catch yourself making the error, when you use the famous undo key (CTRL + Z), the model remains in error state. The best way to resolve this error state is by fixing the problem that caused the error in the first place and then deleting the interest lines on the income statement and reintroducing them. To see this working, follow these steps:

1. Go into the income statement and type some text on one of the projected revenue lines.

	A B	**F**	**G**	**H**	**I**	**J**
		Proj.	Proj.	Proj.	Proj.	Proj.
1	Irene Foods					
2	Income Statement	31-Dec-02	31-Dec-03	31-Dec-04	31-Dec-05	31-Dec-06
3	Net Sales	ed	#VALUE!	#VALUE!	#VALUE!	#VALUE!
4	Clean COGS	#VALUE!	#VALUE!	#VALUE!	#VALUE!	#VALUE!
5	Depreciation	153.5	#VALUE!	#VALUE!	#VALUE!	#VALUE!
6	**Gross profit**	**#VALUE!**	**#VALUE!**	**#VALUE!**	**#VALUE!**	**#VALUE!**
7						
8	SG&A	#VALUE!	#VALUE!	#VALUE!	#VALUE!	#VALUE!
9	Amortisation	0.0	0.0	0.0	0.0	0.0
10	**Operating profit**	**#VALUE!**	**#VALUE!**	**#VALUE!**	**#VALUE!**	**#VALUE!**
11						
12	Non-recurring items	0.0	0.0	0.0	0.0	0.0
13	Interest Income	#VALUE!	#VALUE!	#VALUE!	#VALUE!	#VALUE!
14	Interest Expense	62.6	62.0	61.5	54.8	48.0
15	**Profit before taxes**	**#VALUE!**	**#VALUE!**	**#VALUE!**	**#VALUE!**	**#VALUE!**
16						
17	Taxes	#VALUE!	#VALUE!	#VALUE!	#VALUE!	#VALUE!
18	**Net income**	**#VALUE!**	**#VALUE!**	**#VALUE!**	**#VALUE!**	**#VALUE!**

This introduces an error into the model as the formulae cannot calculate text.

2. Now press CTRL + Z to undo what you just did in order to remove the text. Alternatively, recreate the revenue growth formula.

	A B	F	G	H	I	J
1	Irene Foods	Proj.	Proj.	Proj.	Proj.	Proj.
2	Income Statement	31-Dec-02	31-Dec-03	31-Dec-04	31-Dec-05	31-Dec-06
3	Net Sales	4,876.2	5,217.6	5,582.8	5,973.6	6,391.8
4	Clean COGS	2,691.7	2,880.1	3,081.7	3,297.4	3,528.3
5	Depreciation	153.5	155.2	157.9	161.7	166.4
6	**Gross profit**	**2,031.1**	**2,182.3**	**2,343.2**	**2,514.5**	**2,697.1**
7						
8	SG&A	1,267.8	1,356.6	1,451.5	1,553.1	1,661.9
9	Amortisation	0.0	0.0	0.0	0.0	0.0
10	**Operating profit**	**763.2**	**825.7**	**891.6**	**961.3**	**1,035.2**
11						
12	Non-recurring items	0.0	0.0	0.0	0.0	0.0
13	Interest Income	#VALUE!	#VALUE!	#VALUE!	#VALUE!	#VALUE!
14	Interest Expense	#VALUE!	#VALUE!	#VALUE!	#VALUE!	#VALUE!
15	**Profit before taxes**	**#VALUE!**	**#VALUE!**	**#VALUE!**	**#VALUE!**	**#VALUE!**
16						
17	Taxes	#VALUE!	#VALUE!	#VALUE!	#VALUE!	#VALUE!
18	**Net income**	**#VALUE!**	**#VALUE!**	**#VALUE!**	**#VALUE!**	**#VALUE!**

Everything above the interest line items goes back to normal, but many of the formulae remain in error state. In fact, almost the entire model is in error state!

3. Delete the interest income and interest expense lines in the income statement for the projected years.

	A B	F	G	H	I	J
1	Irene Foods	Proj.	Proj.	Proj.	Proj.	Proj.
2	Income Statement	31-Dec-02	31-Dec-03	31-Dec-04	31-Dec-05	31-Dec-06
3	Net Sales	4,876.2	5,217.6	5,582.8	5,973.6	6,391.8
4	Clean COGS	2,691.7	2,880.1	3,081.7	3,297.4	3,528.3
5	Depreciation	153.5	155.2	157.9	161.7	166.4
6	**Gross profit**	**2,031.1**	**2,182.3**	**2,343.2**	**2,514.5**	**2,697.1**
7						
8	SG&A	1,267.8	1,356.6	1,451.5	1,553.1	1,661.9
9	Amortisation	0.0	0.0	0.0	0.0	0.0
10	**Operating profit**	**763.2**	**825.7**	**891.6**	**961.3**	**1,035.2**
11						
12	Non-recurring items	0.0	0.0	0.0	0.0	0.0
13	Interest Income					
14	Interest Expense					
15	**Profit before taxes**	**763.2**	**825.7**	**891.6**	**961.3**	**1,035.2**
16						
17	Taxes	305.3	330.3	356.6	384.5	414.1
18	**Net income**	**457.9**	**495.4**	**535.0**	**576.8**	**621.1**

The error values disappear!

4. Now undo (CTRL + Z) to reintroduce the interest line items.

	A B	F	G	H	I	J
1	Irene Foods	Proj.	Proj.	Proj.	Proj.	Proj.
2	Income Statement	31-Dec-02	31-Dec-03	31-Dec-04	31-Dec-05	31-Dec-06
3	Net Sales	4,876.2	5,217.6	5,582.8	5,973.6	6,391.8
4	Clean COGS	2,691.7	2,880.1	3,081.7	3,297.4	3,528.3
5	Depreciation	153.5	155.2	157.9	161.7	166.4
6	**Gross profit**	**2,031.1**	**2,182.3**	**2,343.2**	**2,514.5**	**2,697.1**
7						
8	SG&A	1,267.8	1,356.6	1,451.5	1,553.1	1,661.9
9	Amortisation	0.0	0.0	0.0	0.0	0.0
10	**Operating profit**	**763.2**	**825.7**	**891.6**	**961.3**	**1,035.2**
11						
12	Non-recurring items	0.0	0.0	0.0	0.0	0.0
13	Interest Income	5.8	11.1	18.9	24.6	31.1
14	Interest Expense	62.6	62.0	61.5	54.8	48.0
15	**Profit before taxes**	**706.4**	**774.8**	**849.0**	**931.1**	**1,018.3**
16						
17	Taxes	282.6	309.9	339.6	372.5	407.3
18	**Net income**	**423.8**	**464.9**	**509.4**	**558.7**	**611.0**

The model is no longer in error state!

THE ISERROR FUNCTION

The ISERROR function provides a very convenient and user-friendly solution to the error state problem. It saves you from having to run through the steps outlined above. This is especially useful to another user of your model, who may not be very Excel literate!

The ISERROR function returns TRUE if it finds an error and FALSE if it does not find an error. When combined with the IF function, it is a very useful formula.

An integrated model uses the IF and ISERROR functions to return zero if an interest formula goes into error state or to calculate the formula if the interest formula is not in error state. To add this functionality to your model, simply add the ISERROR function to the interest income and interest expense lines on the income statement as shown below:

Interest Income

F13		f_x	=IF(ISERROR(Debt!F80),0,Debt!F80)			
		F	G	H	I	J	K

	A	B	F	G	H	I	J	K
1	Irene Foods		Proj.	Proj.	Proj.	Proj.	Proj.	
2	Income Statement		31-Dec-02	31-Dec-03	31-Dec-04	31-Dec-05	31-Dec-06	
3	Net Sales		4,876.2	5,217.8	5,582.8	5,973.6	6,391.8	
4	Clean COGS		2,691.7	2,860.1	3,081.7	3,297.4	3,528.3	
5	Depreciation		153.5	155.2	157.9	161.7	166.4	
6	**Gross profit**		**2,031.1**	**2,182.3**	**2,343.2**	**2,514.5**	**2,697.1**	
7								
8	SG&A		1,267.8	1,356.6	1,451.5	1,553.1	1,661.9	
9	Amortisation		0.0	0.0	0.0	0.0	0.0	
10	**Operating profit**		**763.2**	**825.7**	**891.6**	**961.3**	**1,035.2**	
11								
12	Non-recurring items		0.0	0.0	0.0	0.0	0.0	
13	Interest Income		5.8	11.1	18.9	24.6	31.1	
14	Interest Expense		62.6	62.0	61.5	54.8	48.0	
15	**Profit before taxes**		**706.4**	**774.8**	**849.0**	**931.1**	**1,018.3**	
16								
17	Taxes		282.6	309.9	339.6	372.5	407.3	
18	**Net Income**		**423.8**	**464.9**	**509.4**	**558.7**	**611.0**	

Interest Expense

F14		f_x	=IF(ISERROR(Debt!F72),0,Debt!F72)			
		F	G	H	I	J	K

	A	B	F	G	H	I	J	K
1	Irene Foods		Proj.	Proj.	Proj.	Proj.	Proj.	
2	Income Statement		31-Dec-02	31-Dec-03	31-Dec-04	31-Dec-05	31-Dec-06	
3	Net Sales		4,876.2	5,217.8	5,582.8	5,973.6	6,391.8	
4	Clean COGS		2,691.7	2,860.1	3,081.7	3,297.4	3,528.3	
5	Depreciation		153.5	155.2	157.9	161.7	166.4	
6	**Gross profit**		**2,031.1**	**2,182.3**	**2,343.2**	**2,514.5**	**2,697.1**	
7								
8	SG&A		1,267.8	1,356.6	1,451.5	1,553.1	1,661.9	
9	Amortisation		0.0	0.0	0.0	0.0	0.0	
10	**Operating profit**		**763.2**	**825.7**	**891.6**	**961.3**	**1,035.2**	
11								
12	Non-recurring items		0.0	0.0	0.0	0.0	0.0	
13	Interest Income		5.8	11.1	18.9	24.6	31.1	
14	Interest Expense		62.6	62.0	61.5	54.8	48.0	

With the ISERROR function included, the model will never go into error state. Something that would normally cause the model to go into error state will simply cause the interest line items on the income statement to zero out. Once the problem is rectified, the model will calculate interest income and expense as normal.

And Finally

CONGRATULATIONS!

Congratulations! You should now have a fully integrated model. Now let's test out the integrity and flexibility of the model.

Let's assume that sales for the company you have modeled decrease by 10% per year during the projection period. Let's also assume that your cost of goods sold % increases, in this case from 55.1% to 60%. Notice that the revolver kicks in for the first projected year as the company requires additional funding. The next two years, despite the company's difficult operating conditions, the company generates excess cash again. Why is this? This is due to the fact that in those two years the company did not need to use cash to pay down very much debt. However, in the fourth projected year, the revolver kicks in again as the company pays down about $200m of debt. This just goes to show how flexible the model is and how important it is to structure the excess cash and revolver lines carefully.

RATIOS

In order to complete your analysis of the business you can add a summary sheet to the model. A typical summary sheet will include key metrics to assess the profitably, financial management and capital efficiency of the business.

	B	C	D	E	F	G	H	
1	Irene Foods	Hist.	Hist.	Hist.	Proj.	Proj.	Proj.	Proj.
2	Summary	31-Dec-99	31-Dec-00	31-Dec-01	31-Dec-02	31-Dec-03	31-Dec-04	31-Dec-05
3	Size							
4	Sales	3,970.9	4,221.0	4,557.2	4,101.5	3,691.4	3,322.2	2,990.0
5	% growth		6.3%	8.0%	(10.0%)	(10.0%)	(10.0%)	(10.0%)
6	Cash flow from operations				217.7	340.2	309.5	277.4
7	Net earnings	460.3	334.5	207.2	224.2	190.0	161.4	132.5
8								
9	Profitability							
10	Gross profit	1,616.2	1,749.8	1,891.7	1,487.1	1,324.0	1,178.7	1,049.2
11	Operating profit	558.4	622.7	621.7	420.7	364.3	314.9	271.8
12	Operating margin	14.1%	14.8%	13.6%	10.3%	9.9%	9.5%	9.1%
13	Net margin	11.6%	7.9%	4.5%	5.5%	5.1%	4.9%	4.4%
14	Return on assets			6.2%	6.9%	6.0%	5.3%	4.6%
15	Return on equity			17.8%	19.1%	15.7%	13.4%	11.5%
16								
17	Leverage & Coverage							
18	Debt to equity			77.1%	78.6%	73.2%	72.9%	78.6%
19	EBIT	558.4	622.7	621.7	420.7	364.3	314.9	271.8
20	EBIT to interest	7.5	8.2	9.0	8.9	7.6	6.8	5.3
21	Eff. Int. Rate (Int. Exp / Avg. Debt)			7.1%	5.6%	5.6%	5.6%	6.2%
22								
23	Asset management							
24	Capital expenditures	140.8	143.0	170.0	143.6	129.2	116.3	104.7

BEAUTY SAVING

Beauty saving is a simple trick to make sure that a user of your model will open it up to the beginning of each work sheet. All you have to do to beauty save is select cell A1 of each worksheet and then save the model.

MODELING STANDARDS

There are a number of standards you should adhere to when building your model. These standards demand that models be:

- Accurate
- Flexible
- User friendly

This section contains some practical advice you should follow in order to adopt these standards:

Accurate: always proof read your model. Make sure you sense check the results. For example, if inventory increases from $100m to $900 for no apparent reason, check that you have not made an error when writing a formula.

Flexible: never use hard numbers in your model. Always make sure that your assumptions are in the assumption area of the model so that you can easily change them if necessary.

User-friendly: break complex calculations down into steps. This will save you from having to write huge formulae that people will not be able to understand!